Praise for *Un:*

"Take courage. Leave fear in the dust. Read *Unshakeable*."

Bob Goff, *New York Times* bestselling author of
Love Does and *Everybody, Always*

"Every now and then, a fresh and younger voice emerges in the world of books, and it is a voice well-worth listening to. Lauren's is such a voice. With refreshing transparency and a contagious love and longing for God, she helps her readers love and long for Jesus more as well. I am one of those readers and I highly recommend *Unshakeable* to you."

Scott Sauls, senior pastor of Christ Presbyterian Church and author of *Jesus Outside the Lines* and *A Gentle Answer*

"Lauren is one of the most truly energetic, dedicated and inspiring people I've met in a long time. The journey she describes in this book is one virtually anyone can relate to—especially if you're in a period of transition in your life. Learn right along with her as she shares vulnerably and courageously a story of growing up, getting out of her own way and discovering the sound of her own voice. As she grows, I know you will too."

Allison Fallon, bestselling author and founder of Find Your Voice

"Lauren will pull you into her journey and give you an upfront view of the many ditches college students and young adults get stuck in, while pointing readers to hope. Lauren reminds you, in the most engaging way, that freedom and redemption are waiting at your doorstep. You're going to love this book!"

Jonathan Pokluda,
author of *Welcome to Adulting*

"Lauren is a natural storyteller who isn't afraid to go first. With honest candor and a willingness to call out her own fears and mistakes, she's the kind of narrator we all want: the kind who takes you by the hand and leads you gently towards the finish line, all the while reminding you of who you are in God's eyes. A story of growing up and growing bold, Lauren's words will inspire you to look at your own story and lean into freedom when the fear is loud."

Hannah Brencher, TED speaker, founder
of More Love Letters, and author of *Come
Matter Here* and *If You Find This Letter*

"College can turn your world upside down. *Unshakeable* helps to turn it right side up. Vulnerable and witty, Lauren leads the way to be courageous and discover who we were always made to be: free."

Pete Hardesty, bestselling co-author of *Adulting 101*

"We all want to have the courage to face hard things. *Unshakeable* serves as a guide to lead others out of fear and into freedom."

Ed Eason, global touring musician and
guitarist for Carrie Underwood

"Lauren's fresh honesty encourages and challenges this emerging generation."

Dale Wallace, executive director of
Vertical Ministries

LAUREN KINNEY

UN
SHAKE
ABLE

OVERCOMING FEAR TO
DISCOVER A LIFE OF FREEDOM

To Jesus.
You change everything.

I keep my eyes always on the LORD.
With Him at my right hand, I will not
be shaken.

Psalm 16:8

CONTENTS

INTRODUCTION

I hate the first four chapters of this book.

Okay, maybe "hate" is too strong of a word. Let's just say that if you could edit your life like you edit a book, I'd edit these right out. They are hard. They are not the picture-perfect moments I wanted to post on Instagram. They don't tell of lifelong friends I was supposed to have by now or my dream college experience.

But of course you can't edit your life. At least not while you're really living it. And while I could edit this book, I suppose, to look the way I think it "should" look, I'm pretty sure I'd lose something in the process.

I have high expectations of myself. Anything outside the perimeter of perfect is not quite perfect. From the way I learned to perfectly form my letters in kindergarten to earning model student awards in elementary school, I've always known how to do it right.

I never wanted to fall short.

I found myself sitting in my living room one rainy Sunday afternoon, laptop in front of me and my copy of the manuscript next to me, staring at the screen blankly. I was sick of re-reading the first four chapters—they told of roommate conflict, breakup tears, questions I didn't have answers for, and things that were wrong I didn't know how to make right. I even told a friend earlier that week that this book would be incredible if I scrapped the first four chapters. Would people shut the book and stick it back on the shelf before they even got to the good parts? And if so, how could I make sure to stay in the "good parts" of my life?

As I sat there, I whispered to God.

"God, I want people to read this book. But I really want people to see You in this book. I'm afraid they won't even get through the first four chapters."

"Lauren," I heard Him say. *"I am present in the first four chapters too."*

I've always imagined God as a Father who gives a squeezy hug when I'm hurting after I've fallen and skinned my knee. My Protector when I lie awake scared in the dark. The One who celebrates me as His child. The kind of Father who holds my hand as we walk through an unfamiliar place.

The first time I ever heard God speak, I was nine years old, riding my bike with one of my younger brothers. It wasn't an audible voice over a loudspeaker, yet was clear and direct in my head. There was no question. I knew who it was.

"Go back, Lauren. Go back."

I pressed down on my brakes on my pink bicycle and yelled at my brother, who was behind me on the sidewalk.

"Conner, we need to go back to the house."

A minute later, we biked into the driveway and there stood my father, holding my youngest brother's body in his arms. His body was black and blue and there was blood everywhere.

My brother had been run over by a truck and I needed to be home.

Since that time, I've found His voice to be one I can trust.

People say God is good at taking something messy and painful and ugly and broken and turning it into something good. Something beautiful. And I believe He can and often does. But things unseen are hard to believe.

I want you to know that God is present in your first four chapters, too. Maybe you're smack in the middle of the first four chapters or you're thriving in your next eight.

But the God who shows up in the next eight is the same God who is redeeming the last four.

To discount painful parts of my story would be to discount God's goodness and grace.

So, right there, on my manuscript, I wrote "He is present in the first four chapters too."

God doesn't ever stop redeeming our story.

I've wondered why I didn't keep a journal while writing this. And then it hit me—the book, the pages you're holding right now, the words you're reading—it is my journal. I am as real in these pages as I would be in person. In fact, I hope it seems like we're sitting across the table having a cup of coffee together. Well, you're drinking coffee and I'm drinking water with lemon. The truth is, I don't even like coffee. I've tried it more than a few times thinking I could teach myself to love it. I mean, milkshakes have cream and sugar, and I like those! My taste buds are just wired for a simple water with lemon.

All of the stories written in front of you are real. I cried a lot while writing them. I didn't want to include some of them. Trust me, I had no plan to tell the world I wet the bed when I was in junior high or admit to anyone I have a love affair with approval and value and success.

But the more real I became, the more Jesus was revealed in my story.

This book was meant for me as much as it was meant for you.

I hope within it you see how Jesus is redeeming your own story, no matter how many bruises you've endured.

My brother had a few broken bones that day when I found

him in my father's arms. And 10 years later, he has some pretty cool scars. But he's okay.

Just like us.

Love,

CHAPTER 1

LETTUCE IS TRAGIC

I married a fish. We had to separate. That can happen when you marry young. I was only nine.

Salmon (as I named him) and I met on the first floor of the church building. (Hey—I know I named a fish after another kind of fish. Give me some grace. I was nine.) I was drawn to the refreshing blue waters and colorful personalities of his other fishy friends.

This was not some informal ordeal. We had a wedding. My sister was the maid of honor and my dad walked me down the carpet hallway covered with Sunday school posters of Jesus and the little children on the walls. One other family was in attendance and generously catered by providing apples and soda. My ring was a Ring Pop—worth far more than a diamond to a nine-year-old. It sounded like the perfect wedding to me.

I marched right up to the tank and said, "I do." And he never had a chance to say no.

I've always been confident in the decisions I've made.

Against the advice of my high school counselor and a few other people smarter than I am, I only applied to one school, and one school only, when searching for a college.

On a rainy, gloomy October day during my junior year of high school, my parents and I drove an hour and a half to Waco, Texas, and four hours later, I knew where I was going to college.

I remember a soft whisper in my heart as I looked out the windows to see the majestic brick buildings disappear as we drove away: *"Lauren, this is where I want you."*

With the same confidence I had when God told me to "go back" after my brother's accident, I knew whose voice I was hearing.

What resulted was a mix of relief and excitement and fear all at the same time. I know God makes all things possible and this would be no exception, but it still made me nervous. God continued to reaffirm my place at Baylor the more I visited during my junior and senior years of high school, whether I was meeting with a dean in the business school, exploring dorms or with friends at a football game. He continued to whisper the same thing to my anxious heart: *"Lauren, this is where I want you."*

I wanted to listen. And yet the thought of leaving everything I knew made me sick.

Senior year flew by and I walked across the stage at graduation in front of my wildly cheering family and friends I had known since third grade. Summer seemed to be a blink. The countdown to move-in went from double digits to single digits, and with every passing day, I was more and more anxious and lying through my teeth when people started asking right and left if I were ready. "Yes, I'm so excited!" I would exclaim, when in reality I wanted to throw up at the thought of leaving a place comfortably familiar to me.

I had never been so anxious about anything and I couldn't understand why. My friends weren't like this, and they were headed to places much further than Waco. It only made me angrier at myself. Falling asleep proved challenging. I longed for a switch that could turn off my churning mind. Trips to the toilet proved useless: nothing but dry heaves. When I did sleep, I would startle awake, shaking, crying and short of breath—panicked and in fear. It didn't matter where I went or who I was with or what I was doing. Fear began to grip every part of my life for almost two months.

My boyfriend at the time and I were about to celebrate

two years of dating before we left for college. Jake and I met on a volleyball court in Minneapolis, but we weren't playing. Our sisters were. Our families traveled together to tournaments and over time we became good friends. The hours we spent watching our sisters play volleyball in many states set the stage for my first real dating relationship. And he drove a Jeep. He was cool.

I drove to Jake's house one morning so that he could take me to breakfast at one of our favorite places: Waffle House. I sobbed the full 17 minutes to his house. My car came to a stop, and I was thankful I had a nice stash of napkins to wipe my mascara-stained face. I took a deep breath, stepped out of my car onto the sidewalk and lost it. I cleaned myself up once again and told myself to get it together and rang the doorbell.

I hadn't even made it five minutes before I started crying again as we drove out of his neighborhood. I remember sitting at a stoplight and praying so hard God would help me get myself together so I could spend some quality time with Jake without looking like someone had thrown a water balloon in my face. I thought I had at least partially gotten myself together, but the moment we walked inside our favorite yellow building, I lost it all over again.

I could not stop sobbing at Waffle House. Like ugly crying.

Snotty nose and everything. My hands reached up to hide my face in pure humiliation. Jake was so kind and offered me more napkins, but I could tell he was embarrassed. So there we sat on the sticky black swirly chairs at the bar at Waffle House. There was Jake, calmly eating his waffle. And then there was me, sobbing over my egg whites and sausage patties. And then there was our waiter, who kept handing me napkins and politely asking me why I was crying, even though I didn't even know why. I couldn't live like this anymore. Fear of the unknown consumed me. It was terrifying and exhausting and humiliating. I walked around ready to explode into tears any instant. None of my friends seemed to be struggling. I couldn't understand why this was happening to me.

This wasn't me.

I was the confident decision-maker. I knew exactly what I wanted and where I wanted to go. I knew what I was studying and what I was going to accomplish. I knew what it was supposed to look like and how I was supposed to act.

This wasn't me.

I had done a good job of hiding the mess I had become. Remember that store in the mall where you could stuff your own teddy bear? I was an expert at stuffing and stuffing my unkempt emotion and neatly closing it all up inside.

I'd like to say I wasn't aware of my unsettled fear of the

future, but deep down it was undeniable. There was this part of me that had a feeling I wouldn't be the same person anymore after driving south down I-35 to be in Waco. Maybe that's why I was so scared and panicked. Home was familiar territory, and college was not. I loved the calm of my neighborhood. I sat at the same table at the local coffee shop. I knew where the closest Chick-fil-A and Target were. Waco was new, and new was uncomfortable. Very uncomfortable. Every time I thought of it, I felt sick to my stomach.

But like I had always done, I told myself I just needed to suck it up and get to Waco.

On my last night with my childhood best friend, Melody, before we left for college, I gave her a scrapbook. Inside were notes I had written to her over the course of five years. Notes that encompassed memories from years of friendship.

In those pages you could have found evidence of every crush from elementary to high school, late night talks over ice cream, volleyball try-outs each August, and wisdom teeth anesthesia laughs. I remember standing in the parking lot of our go-to frozen yogurt shop and handing it to her as we said "see you later" with tears running all down our faces. The moment she took it from my hands, it all became real. I was saying goodbye to all the years I had been known and loved and trading them for four more I was afraid wouldn't know me or love me back.

My friend has what she likes to call the "all is lost" moments. I think these are moments in life when you feel stripped away from everything and all is falling right through your hands and shattering into a million tiny pieces. Super glue can't even do the job anymore. The funny thing about "all is lost" moments is this: often, everything is just coming together. Driving down to Waco that mid-August early morning in my car packed with boxes, I was driving into my biggest "all is lost" moment yet.

I was about to lose something I had never lost before: control.

Jake and I celebrated our two-year anniversary the day before I left for Baylor, and somehow I was able to keep it together. He was a familiar comfort, and yet something in me knew he was one more thing that wouldn't be the same after that night. Move-in day came, and I held back my tears successfully until my family made one last trip to Target.

I broke down in the produce aisle standing next to the lettuce.

Lettuce can seem very tragic when you're learning to let go.

• • •

Then it was October.

It had been two months since student volunteers unloaded my car and carried all my brown boxes into a plain dorm room with white walls that was now my home. Two months since I had forgotten to bring pillows for my bed, leaving me sobbing next to the lettuce bin at Target. Totally normal. School was in full swing and hard, but it wasn't what I was thinking about. The anxiety hadn't gone away, and I was angry. Angry I was lonely in a place that abounded with people. Angry that my life wasn't reflecting my college dream. I'd always imagined campus as a flood of people with smiles sewn on their faces—and I never thought mine wouldn't be one of them. I was angry I couldn't sleep at night. Each day I watched with wonder and a little bit of jealousy as my friends found their places and their friends, and the steady stream of posed Instagram pictures never failed to stir the pot of loneliness.

I thought I would be fine by now. Maybe I heard wrong. If God were here, if He saw me, knew me, heard me, surely this— this college dream that has turned into a nightmare—would not be happening. He never told me it was going to be this way.

But I knew I could trust the voice that had told me one day, all of those years ago, to "go back." I knew I could trust the voice that told me Baylor was my place.

Sometimes everything has to be stripped away for us to discover who we are and what we're made of.

• • •

One fall day, I found myself standing outside my dorm waiting for a grey Honda to pick me up. The orange and brown leaves swirled around me and the wind blew through my ponytail as I leaned my body against the railing. It was the beauty of fall, and yet I was too busy to notice. I was thinking about the test I would stay up late studying for and replaying a conversation I had with someone earlier.

There was me, in clear focus, and the rest of the world around me in a smeared blur.

Jason pulled up, snapping me out of my daydream and back into reality. We had gone to high school together, but hadn't become friends until I got to Baylor. Jason had quickly become a steady voice of truth. He was one of the few people who saw past my facade into my brokenness. I hopped in the backseat, reserving the front for our friend Austin, who was also going with us to Bible study. Austin and I had been friends since third grade, where he was my elementary school crush. After a few minutes, Austin came sprinting outside and Jason and I may or may not have rolled our eyes.

We were going to be late—again. Austin's feet thundered down the concrete stairway. He swung open the front door, jumped in the front seat, and we were off. I had sent Austin an encouraging text that morning and started to tease him about not responding back.

Suddenly Jason waved his hand in the air, and Austin and I were silent. "Guys. Austin showed me this song and it's wrecked me." Music flooded Jason's speakers and we listened. The chorus struck me:

God, You don't need me
But somehow You want me
Oh, how You love me
Somehow that frees me
To take my hands off of my life
And the way it should go

God, You don't need me
But somehow You want me
Oh, how You love me
Somehow that frees me
To open my hands up
And give You control
I give You control.[1]

Jason and Austin sang so loudly, and I remember sitting in the backseat, watching as Jason kept trying to drive and open his hands in worship at the same time. Tears filled our eyes, and we smiled. Jason, Austin and I were each fighting different battles that night. The battles were invisible to everyone but the three of us.

That song by Tenth Avenue North reminded us of the one thing we already knew but needed to believe again: true freedom in Jesus comes when we give up control. At that point, I could not have cared less about being late or the test I had in the morning, or the hard conversation I'd had earlier that day. What mattered was the truth that we so badly needed to hear. And that we were in this together.

After grabbing Sonic drinks and having our normal theological debates on the way home, Jason dropped off Austin and me. As we walked the quarter-mile back to our dorm, I wondered if this was what college was supposed to feel like. I could hear Austin and Jason's laughter, and as the chorus of the song replayed in my head, I sighed and smiled. Maybe this was college. Hard but real. Never pretty, but worth it when you have people fighting beside you.

God began teaching me two things that week. First, we have to lose control of the things we grip most tightly if we truly trust who God says He is. My tightly clenched, sweaty hands are no match for His safe, holy hands. In no way do I deserve His unwavering, relentless pursuit of my heart, so why am I not giving Him everything I have in return?

Second, it's okay to ask why. God is teaching me that it's okay to ask questions. We have the beautiful freedom to ask anything and everything 24/7, 365 days a year. He never condemns the questions, no matter how hard, but longs for His kids to simply ask. He's constantly reminding me, *"Lauren, it's okay not to know because I know it all."* We can ask all the questions we want, but all He asks is that we trust Him.

My friend Emma and I have talked about this. Both of us had broken hearts over broken relationships, but Emma was actively choosing to seek Jesus anyway. In between a spoonful of her soup at dinner one night, she blurted out, "People tell me all the time, 'Wow, Emma. That's so awesome and mature how you're choosing to lean into Jesus during this time.'"

She paused and looked at me. "Lauren, what other choice did I have? I tried every other way, person and thing. And they failed. But Jesus was there every single time. Why would I run anywhere else? I didn't have anywhere else to go."

Isn't this what we find time and time again? We frequently find ourselves running *back* to Him. Maybe we should've run to Him first?

If you let go, you'll gain a better grip.

CHAPTER 2

RUNNING AWAY

The night Jason and Austin and I bonded over a single song, I walked back into my dorm and immediately didn't want to be there. Once I opened the door, it was like every feeling of loneliness and anxiety and fear I had left behind before getting into Jason's car that night slapped me in the face, screaming, "Did you miss me?"

I changed into my favorite pajama pants and an old T-shirt and flipped open my computer to stream the MLB Wild Card game—a distraction to numb the pain and loneliness. But of course it wasn't available to stream. So instead, I opened Spotify to play the only song I had heard all night— "Control." The melody rang into my ears and I began crying again, even though I wasn't sure exactly why. I asked my roommate Sydney, who was in her bed studying, if I could turn off the lights. She gave me a sideways look but said yes anyway and clicked the switch to turn on her lamp. I didn't want her to see me cry.

Sydney and I had known each other three years before becoming roommates at Baylor. We didn't hang out in the same crowd, so we were more acquaintances than friends. Sydney was quiet, smart and killed it in pre-calculus. I needed a roommate and so did she. In my mind, this couldn't be more perfect. What could possibly go wrong? I figured out quickly we were more different than I thought—and that learning to live with someone who is different than you was a bigger task than I imagined.

Not wanting to explain myself, I sat on the hard ground in our tiny closet and could feel a darkness, a heaviness in the room.

The Bible says in 1 Peter 5:8, "Your enemy the devil prowls around like a roaring lion looking for someone to devour."

His roar erupted.

You're alone, Lauren. You're worthless. You'll never amount to anything. You need control to save your life. You really believe losing control will help you? It will make this worse.

I shook my head. The lies were familiar—the enemy had been taunting me with them since I left home. I sat cross-legged in our closet that was separated from our room by a white curtain. The song played over and over and over again in my headphones and I held my hands out to God the entire time—a way to physically symbolize what I was trying to do: give Him control. My body shook with the fear of what this meant. I wanted so desperately to know the freedom the song talked about. The freedom to lose control completely to a Father who loves me and would take my fear and pierce it with His love. I knew He would show up. I knew He would come.

After what felt like hours, I pulled back the closet curtain and climbed into bed, silently begging God for just an hour of sleep. I was restless. Exhausted. Where was that switch for me to turn my mind off? I hadn't been able to sleep the night before and I had a feeling this would be no different. I closed my eyes but my mind kept racing and racing. All I wanted was to be still. To be free.

Midnight, my phone read. I laid there, in silence, listening in angst to Sydney breathe peacefully, and staring at the ceiling in the darkness. 12:20.

I have to leave.

I threw my phone charger to the side of my bed, slipped Birkenstocks on, and grabbed my keys. The door clicked quietly behind me and I stepped out into the lonely carpeted hallway.

Where do I go?

My heart beat faster and faster, and my hands trembled as I dialed a phone number I knew would get answered. Rebecca picked up on the second ring, and I made my way to my car, street lamps illuminating my way even in the pitch-black darkness of the night.

Five minutes later, I was standing on the cold, hard tile inside Rebecca's house, wrapped in a blanket, while she prayed and ran her fingers through my hair. Rebecca was like an older sister to me. Our families lived a mile and a half from each other, and I spent many days after school playing in her family's ping-pong tournaments or swimming in their backyard pool. I knew I could call her in the middle of the night and she would let me sleep on her couch. We all need a friend like that.

I woke up that morning on a couch in her living room. And for the first time all week, I had actually slept.

Sydney was still sleeping when I walked in the room the next morning. I changed quietly out of my pajamas, grabbed my laptop and backpack, and walked over to the campus coffee shop. The past 10 hours had been a complete blur and I knew if I did nothing the rest of the world was going to become blurry too. I ordered a drink, fell into a couch, and did the only thing I knew how to do: write.

You are safe.

I have won.

The victory is Mine,

This is My battle.

Not yours.

You are safe.

You are not alone.

I am here.

I am with you.

Be still, Lauren.

I am here.

Be still. You are not alone.

You were never alone.

Hide in Me.

Find your refuge in Me.

I am here.

I am fighting for you.

I have fought for you.

And I have won for you.

I have won.

The battle is Mine and I have won.

The cross has the final word.

I have won, Lauren.

As I chewed on my straw, my fingers flew across the keyboard recounting every detail of the entire evening— the unbearable weight of the enemy's lies in contrast to the overwhelming peace and sleep at Rebecca's house. I shook my head. *How?* I wondered. *Why was Rebecca still up?* Even she had admitted when I got there that she never stayed up that late.

An hour flew by and it was time for class. My mouse reached for the upper left-hand corner to save the document. *Save As…?* my computer asked. My fingers froze on the keyboard. What word could possibly encompass the past 12 hours? My left index finger reached for the "F" and I let it type. 'F-R-E-E-D-O-M,' it typed. I closed the lid of my computer and shoved it back into my backpack. I froze. *Freedom? Why in the world did I just name it "freedom"?*

I wiggled my straw deep into the pile of ice that had gathered at the bottom of my plastic cup and took one last sip of iced tea and lemonade. An hour before, the sun was just beginning to wake up. Now it shone so brightly, even making the weeds on the sidewalk look like plants beginning to bloom. I brought my hand up to shield my eyes and stepped out onto the sidewalk. I was coming out of hiding with them.

God, I began to pray as I walked to class. *I don't know what You're doing or where You are, but I know this is only the beginning. Help me fight.*

I heard His voice as clear as the sky above me.

"I don't abandon My children, Lauren."

• • •

I'm afraid of the dark. I have been since I was a kid, but my fear escalated more and more when I was in junior high and high school. Locking myself in the darkness became a form of punishment whenever I disappointed myself or the people around me. I would close my windows, turn off the lights, and shove myself up against a wall to sit in a corner. Some nights I would come home and make myself shower in the dark. I hated it, but I felt like I deserved it. Next time I would do better and whatever had happened would not happen again.

One night I stayed in a hotel with my mom and sister. Before we went to bed, my mom rolled down the window shade so that the room was pitch black. All throughout the night, I woke up shaking in fear from nightmares and the looming darkness. I slid out of bed and tip-toed over to the couch in the corner. I began to pray that the enemy would leave, that God would protect our room, and that light would infiltrate the darkness. After two hours, the sun began peeking through the shade and light shone throughout the room. I will never forget the feeling of relief as I watched the sun stream through the window and I heard His voice.

"I am a rescuer, Lauren."

That's kind of how I felt that night at Rebecca's—like I'd found that sliver of sunlight that would give me freedom.

• • •

I've heard the best writers write to a person. Not to an audience. A person. A living, breathing person.

"So, who are you writing this book to?" Ally asked. She's a writer I admire and a mentor to me in the writing process.

We were sitting in her small home right on the outskirts of LA one morning. The windows surrounding her house were an open invitation to the sun, which flooded into the room and made the words on the giant sticky notes on the wall pop off the paper. They were coming alive in the light. We both threw out a few names, and nothing felt right. Ally paused. "What about your roommate?" The suggestion seemed audacious. After a long pause and a deep breath, I looked at Ally and smiled. Actually, Sydney was the perfect person to write to. Deep down, I think we all want to be understood.

I set a rule for myself during my first semester of college:

I couldn't go home for a month. I think the rule was made with good intentions. I wanted to adjust to my new life at college and knew I could not if I were leaving all the time. But I am often good at assuming the rules I follow are the rules the people *around* me should follow. And the bottom line is that this was a self-imposed rule that applied to nobody but me.

I'll never forget the first time Sydney left to go home for the weekend. I was so jealous—so jealous she had the freedom to leave while I felt I did not. Loneliness consumed me that weekend, and the enemy once again began pelting me with the lie that I wasn't worth anything.

You don't have any friends.

No one cares about you.

God lied to you.

After one month had passed, I broke my own rule and rushed home. That's when I realized why Sydney had been running away every weekend. Home meant safety and familiarity. I had been so quick to assume her story. To assume she simply wasn't courageous enough to stay. When all along, she was running towards home—the one place filled with the people that kept her coming back to the place that left her empty.

There was just so much I didn't realize then and so much I realize now. Sydney left to be loved—kind of like I did. So of course it made sense to write to a person who, despite our differences, understood my struggle.

An Open Letter:

Dear Sydney,

I realize now that we were both fighting invisible battles, but let me explain. Here's why I left that night:

The enemy's roar was deafening. Sleep was failing. I was sure you would not understand.

I came back early that morning and you were still asleep, so I shut our door as quietly as I could and grabbed some clothes and changed in the dark. When I saw you later that afternoon, I told you what had happened, leaving out as many details as I could. I didn't want to scare you or think it was your fault or that I was crazy, because it probably sounded like I was.

When I told you I had stayed the night at Rebecca's, you stared blankly at me. I remember thinking, *She has no idea the invisible battle I'm fighting.* I was right. But I had no idea you were fighting one too.

Remember that monthly women's gathering I told you about? On that particular night, I didn't want to go. It had been a rough day, school was kicking my butt, and we were avoiding each other. I don't know why, but I decided to go anyway. A white tissue blotted the dripping mascara off my face and before getting out of my car in the church parking lot, I checked my mirror to make sure no one would be able to tell I had been crying. I grabbed my Bible and my notebook in the seat next to me and prayed as I walked up the steep stairwell.

God, would you just let someone notice me?

Who comes to college to feel like this? I said to myself. *I'm a total wimp. Is this really what I've come to?*

I walked in the doors confident. This was a place where surely someone would notice me. I plastered a small smile on my face and looked up to greet the ladies at the front doors, but they were already talking to other people. *No worries,* I thought to myself. There would be someone else. I made my way to the seats in the worship center and sat down on a row with a few people, but they were checking Instagram on their phones. Not one of them glanced up in my direction.

A man on stage began strumming his guitar and lyrics flashed on the screen. My mouth began moving but I wasn't singing the words. "I'm not invisible. I'm not invisible," I started repeating to myself. I don't remember exactly when, but sometime between the end of worship and the sermon, I left. Holding back tears, I walked out the double doors and into the parking lot and sat sobbing as soon as I shut the door to my car.

No. No. I refused to believe it. I wasn't invisible. That night, I hadn't shown up looking for another Bible verse or worship song or prayer. I just wanted a hug. A conversation. A "Hello, we're glad you're here." I just wanted to be seen.

I wonder if that's how you felt too, and I'm sorry if I ever made you feel that way. I think we would both agree that freshman year at Baylor was one of the most difficult years of our lives, but I won't ever be able to imagine it without you. And I'm grateful for that. Thanks for putting up with all my late concerts and weird dance moves and all the times I burned popcorn and you walked into a smoky room. I know you didn't exactly like it when you would come back from taking a shower and I was playing loud music and flipping the light switch back and forth like our room was a dance party for one. I know you lost a lot of sleep every time I woke you up from coming home in the early hours of the morning.

I'm proud of you. Finding who you were took you longer than you thought, but you fought anyway. You refused to let the year be a waste and finished with a 4.0 GPA. You refused to let a place you disliked become a place of defeat.

You ran. I ran. But all along we were really running from the same thing.

I remember the day we got our Business 101 final grades. I

was eating cereal in the dining hall when my mouth dropped in horror. I bombed it. Completely unexpected. I threw my dirty dishes on the conveyer belt and wondered where to go to cry. I turned towards the stairs leading to our hallway and stopped. You were up there, and I knew you were going to ask me how I did. I knew you did better than I, so I ran across the parking lot and got in my car and called my dad instead.

Later that night, you asked me how I did. I glanced down at the floor and told you. "How did you do?" I asked in return. A number fell out of your mouth, and I nearly laughed. You had done worse than I. I don't remember what we did that night, but I think both of us fell asleep smiling. On that same night explaining why I left, I thought, *Can we really understand each other when we are so different? Is it even worth trying?*

But all along, we were fighting the same battle. The times trying to talk to you seemed more hopeless than promising, and I know you felt the same way about me. Your words hurt me, and mine hurt you. But somehow, we would often find ourselves sitting at Chick-fil-A eating kid's meals together.

I was there when you decided to change your major to art history. Decided to buy the cycling class fitness pass that you actually used but I never did. Decided to move. Decided to leave behind your two closest friends you had grown up with. Decided to transfer.

You are so brave. I just wish I would have told you to your face.

In your brokenness, I saw the cracks and bruises and hurts of my own heart. In your joy, I saw small things that were worth sitting an hour in the Whataburger drive-thru at midnight to celebrate.

I wanted nothing to do with our differences, but now it's only through our differences that I see growth. God used our brokenness, together, to be a catalyst for strength and refinement and big dreams.

You taught me grace. (Even when I broke your bottle of salad dressing.)

You taught me compassion.

You are far from perfect, but so am I.

You taught me how to fight. And how to win.

I am so thankful you're a part of my story.

CHAPTER 3

GOOD GIRL REBEL

The weekend I learned to loosen my grip—*that* was the weekend. I ran home. To break up with Jake.

I sat there at Starbucks, 30 minutes early, waiting for him to walk through the door. My laptop sat open on the table in front of me to give the illusion that I was working, but my fingers didn't get the memo, refusing to type, sweating and slipping across the keyboard. I had no idea what Jake was coming to say, but I knew I was going to break up with him.

We were at different schools. Labor Day had seemed like the perfect time to see each other. I didn't realize how much emotional distance the physical distance had put between us. The silence was a bit startling as we sat at our favorite restaurant. We didn't talk like we used to.

The week before I was sitting at that Starbucks, I had

spent hours typing up this long explanation of why I was making this decision to break up and that I still wanted to be friends and a bunch of other sugarcoated nonsense by a non-confrontation queen. We sat down at a table outside and I pulled the two sheets of paper out of my backpack as my hands shook in fear. Jake started laughing at me.

"You typed it up, didn't you?"

He smiled. I nervously laughed and began to read my script I had so painstakingly prepared. I wasn't even two sentences in when Jake looked at me.

"Lauren, I'm breaking up with you too."

My serious face changed into a smile and I threw my well-written script back into my bag and leaned back into my chair. For the next hour, Jake and I sat and talked. As friends. I think about that moment now and realize God was teaching me even then that I could feel lonely, but I wasn't alone.

It was painful. It felt like He was stripping me of every good thing in my life, when in reality He wanted me to realize He is the only good, perfect person in my life. God was gently asking me to trade my loneliness and trust Him. He wanted me to stop supergluing the hole in my heart and start filling it with something I had failed to recognize: His love.

• • •

It was a chilly day in Waco. I had finally pulled out my long, fuzzy socks and warm sweatshirt that nearly covered my knees and my hands were nestled inside the pockets of my warm jacket. I was walking briskly, probably too close past the fountain as cold water sprinkled across my cheek. I saw her coming and wanted to avoid her, but I was running late to class and taking another route would make me even later. I looked up and we made eye contact, and there was no turning away. I smiled and slowed down my pace.

"Hey Lauren!"

"Hey Marissa! How are you?" I asked.

I liked Marissa. We sat next to each other in a class my freshman year. She was always direct—you never had to wonder what she was thinking. She had known I had been going home more frequently, and I knew she disapproved. But that morning, I simply was not in the mood to hear it.

As the wind blew her long, blonde ponytail she responded, "I'm doing good! How's your semester going?"

I really was not in the mood. I don't know why, but for some reason, I was honest. I was tired of putting on a fake smile and blurting out the overused "I'm good!" It was a lie. I was not good. I was not okay.

"Actually, it's been hard. This isn't what I thought it would be. I'm pretty sure Sydney's transferring…" I trailed off. She ended my sentence for me. "Well, maybe you should think about it too!" she said while waving to another person walking past us. "I gotta go, catch you later!" Without a word, I placed my tumbler back in my backpack and walked into my history class right on time.

The rest of the week, I replayed our conversation over and over again. I tried to think of some adequate response had she not walked away so quickly, but I could only come up with four words. *If only you knew. If only you knew*, I wanted to scream back at her hurtful comment about transferring. She had no idea.

From the outside, it must have looked like I was running. Running away from the workload. Running away from the pressure. The anxiety. The loneliness. Running in fear. But to me, there was an internal war being fought that no one knew about. And every time I stepped foot on campus, it was like entering a war zone where my white flag was already on display.

I sat across from people every week who would smile and sip their coffee and look me in the eye and say with the kindest of voices, "Lauren, maybe you should just try staying in town for once. Just one time." They would grab me gently by the shoulders and smile, and then hug me and I knew the conversation was over. Stay, they would say. Just try staying.

As if it would solve everything with a snap of a finger. Oh, I wish it would have. But they had no idea how deep, deep, deep the roots were. Like Sydney, it was the people I was running home to that gave me the courage to *run* back and fight harder.

Here's what I wanted them to understand: leaving isn't always running away. Most of the time people are just running towards something else.

• • •

When we were in high school, every Sunday night at seven my sister and I would drive ten minutes to Bible study. All the high school girls would gather at a host home for double-stuffed Oreos, gooey brownies, and worship. Halfway through the evening, we broke up into our assigned groups and headed to our spot in the house to discuss the lesson. On this particular Sunday night, my family had gotten home from one of my sister's 12-hour volleyball tournaments. We had been up since 5:30 that morning and Hannah and I were both ready to crash on the couch when our car pulled into the driveway.

Hannah is my favorite human ever. We've been best friends since she was born, when I was two years old. From her infamous letter to me that started with "Dear Poopy Pants…"

to the time we sat on the cold tile of our kitchen floor and drank pickle juice from the jar through two straws, Hannah has been my sister shenanigans partner-in-crime since I can remember. She's slept with me through every thunderstorm, I've cleaned up her puke, and we never missed the chance to belt out every line of Justin Bieber's "Baby" with jumbo cherry limeades in our hands. Really, all of our adventures could fill an encyclopedia-sized book.

That night, despite our exhausted looks, my dad insisted Hannah and I go to Bible study anyway. The scowl on my face showed it all.

"Are you joking?"

He was not.

When it was time to leave, Hannah came to the door where I was impatiently waiting, wearing none other than my sweatshirt. "Did you *ask* to wear that?" I sneered in typical big-sister fashion. "Take it off."

She stormed away to her room, her feet thundering all the way up the wooden stairs. I walked out to my car and checked my clock. We were going to be late. No surprise. Hannah swung open the passenger door and slid into the leather seat with a look on her face that I was well-familiar with: "I really don't want to be mad at you, but you're not backing down so neither will I." Her blonde curls turned to the window, refusing to look at me. I didn't want to look at her either, so in our stubborn nature we sat in silence.

I took the right turn into the neighborhood and broke the 10 minutes of silence with wailing tears. "I hate this. I hate being here. This is not where I find myself." The moment I walked into the door, I would be met with the same fake smiles once again. Every week we sat in the same circle and said the same things about who God was and that He was faithful and good and everything would be okay, and I was sick of it. Bible study was supposed to be a real environment, where each person could be *real*. And yet, as I looked around at the superficial smiling faces in the circle, I could tell we were holding things back. I was tired of settling for fake faces in fake places.

I just wanted something real. Someone real.

I pulled the car over in front of the house and made a decision. I wasn't getting out. "We're not going," I announced. Hannah's jaw dropped. I whipped my car into reverse and sped out of the neighborhood, praying silently that none of my friends would be coming the opposite direction and recognize my car.

I reached the stoplight a few blocks away and turned and looked over at Hannah. The silence broke and we began laughing so hard I started crying all over again. Together, we reached down and picked up the lesson sheets for the night and tore them to shreds all over my car floor. Thirty minutes later, as I sat across from Hannah sipping my water with lemon at our favorite restaurant, it hit me. I just ran away from *Bible study*—the ultimate sin. Did Jesus really die for that too? Tearing up Bible study lesson sheets was never addressed in the youth group.

As I ate my sandwich and Hannah spread butter on her baked potato, we talked about real things. Broken relationships and things we didn't want Mom and Dad to know. How God felt far away more than He felt close. The questions we were asking Him that no one at Bible study was talking about.

On the way home, we debated how my dad was going to handle our rebellious actions. I was fully prepared to take the full blame for it. I didn't care. This was real.

Jesus met Hannah and me right where we were that night—at the stoplight shredding blue discussion sheets that littered the floor of my car. And He didn't run. He isn't afraid of our honest questions. He isn't afraid of our disappointments or the things we want to hide. When life is messy, He does the exact opposite of what we think He will do. He runs towards us, not away from us.

Two hours later, we pulled into the driveway and slowly opened the door. My dad got up from his chair in front of the computer and hugged us as we walked inside. "I'm glad y'all are home. How was it tonight?"

My shoulders straightened and my face tightened. I was ready to defend my actions with a perfect explanation. My dad had no idea what was coming. His eyes met mine and as I fearlessly declared our actions, I prepared myself for the worst.

I expected punishment. Maybe my phone would be snatched for the week or I would wave a tearful goodbye to my car keys.

This time my jaw dropped at the words that fell out of his mouth. "Sounds like y'all had fun!" he answered with a huge smile on his face.

Rather than passing out punishment, he served us a platter of grace. So much grace. Grace that came spinning like a curveball I never saw coming. Grace I wasn't expecting and grace I didn't deserve. We had rebelled. We weren't where we were supposed to be. Yet the kindness in my dad's blue eyes said "Hey. I see you. I see you right where you are and what you've done and I'm going to love you anyway. Because you're my daughter and I call you mine."

My Father says the same: *"You're My daughter and I call you Mine."*

No matter what.

• • •

Two years later, I found myself running again. Running from the illusion of thriving in college and the harsh reality that I wasn't. It was never supposed to be this way. I was supposed to marry that guy from high school, have dance parties with my roommate, be in a church small group, and eat healthy and run five miles every other day. I was supposed to be thriving.

Instead I was the girl who went home nearly every weekend, desperately searching for a place where I could trade loneliness for love. Real love. Where someone actually loved me back.

I found it at home. This was a place where anxiety's attacks would be met with a force of overpowering love. I'd barely make it through the week, come home, and somehow my dad and I would end up in a drive-thru somewhere and he would give me a pep talk. "Lauren, I am proud of you," he would say. I would turn my head to the right in a terrible attempt to hide the tears that trickled down my face. I didn't deserve to hear those words. Late Sunday night I would drive back and then start the process all over again. My parents never told me to stay at Baylor. They never refused to let me come home. Every time I'd call in tears announcing I was on my way, my mom would give me the same answer: "This is still your home, and you are always welcome here."

I ran. But someone else was running after me too.

. . .

My first wreck wasn't my fault. I had just picked up a friend and we were headed to Dallas for church on a Tuesday night. My car was stopped in a double turn lane when the truck behind me hit the brakes too late. I didn't even feel the movement—I only heard the sound.

There happened to be an inlet just past the turn, so I immediately pulled over and watched in my rearview mirror for the man in the truck to do the same. But instead, he zipped past me and onto the highway. Without a second thought, I threw my car into drive, turned around, and merged onto the highway.

Those 30 seconds are still a blur—my heart was racing and my hands were shaking. The adrenaline rush was real, and I wasn't going to let this guy get away. A few minutes later, I spotted the truck to my right on an access road just off the highway. My friend grabbed her phone and began taking pictures of the truck while I called 9-1-1 and asked what to do. I guess I expected some motivational speech from the operator with dramatic music in the background, but to my surprise, the operator told me to stop pursuing the vehicle and pull over.

"Are you kidding me?" I nearly said into my phone. "Ma'am, he just hit me." The operator didn't think it was funny. "You're putting yourself, your passenger, and the cars around you at risk by pursuing the vehicle," she said.

She was right. I exited off the highway, pulled over into a nearby parking lot, and got out to assess the damage. It wasn't pretty, but it could have been a whole lot worse. My friend and I weren't hurt, and the car was drivable. Our night wasn't about to be ruined by some random dude and a hit-and-run, so we hopped back in the car and drove to church.

All this time I've been running, Jesus was running after me. But this chase is different. Jesus doesn't ever pull over to assess the damage we've done. He is not afraid of the messes we've made. I think He would rather us tell Him what we're really thinking rather than putting on a fake smile like everything is okay. We might run. He keeps sprinting. He chases after us until our legs give out, and we fall into His extended arms as He says, *"I am still your Father and you are always welcome here."*

CHAPTER 4

NOT MADE FOR BUSINESS PANTS

At a young age, I learned that being different made you weak.

I wet the bed until I was 12 years old. And let me tell you, it's mortifying to shop in the diaper aisle when you're 12. My younger brothers, who were six and eight at the time, didn't understand why I was years older than they were and wearing pull-ups to bed at night. I didn't understand either. It wasn't my fault I was different.

I was in junior high when my parents made a crazy decision to send my siblings and I to a camp a few states away. It seemed like everyone we knew had gone to this camp and had the best time of their lives. One night our family gathered around the dinner table eating tacos on paper plates, and my parents announced that the four of us were going in the summer—and we didn't have a choice. On the laptop on our wooden table, I saw smiling faces of campers and counselors jumping off inflatables, flying in the air, and splashing into a swimming pool below. It looked awesome, but it had been a while since I'd gone to camp overnight. I was hesitant.

The month of June quickly approached. My mom bought my siblings and I big black trunks with silver buckles to pack our stuff in, and I was sure I would never use it again. I was right. Four full trunks later, we closed the garage behind us and began the 10-hour drive. Our white Suburban pulled through the gates, and I watched as the pictures I had seen online months before came alive before my eyes. Counselors were screaming and waving their hands in the air, smiling and laughing. I silently hoped that I would love it.

On the second night, my group was gathered in our teepee getting ready to go to bed when my two counselors approached me.

"Hey Lauren! Could we talk outside?" they echoed in unison.

They tried to make it really discreet, but the rest of the 12-year-old girls turned around and looked at me like I was in some sort of trouble. I opened the flap to the teepee and we stepped outside. I stood there silently, replaying my day in my head, trying to remember if I had said or done anything that would have put me in this situation.

The blonde counselor spoke first. "Lauren, we don't mean this to be awkward or anything, but we were told that you have a problem wetting the bed." The brunette counselor nodded and interjected, "But we don't want this to be awkward or anything. I wet the bed a few times when I was little too." My face went bright red and I looked down at my pink swim shoes that were covered in mud. I hoped they didn't notice. "I'm taking medicine for it," I whispered. I didn't know what else to say.

"We just wanted to make sure that you knew we knew about it and that it will stay between us." I looked up at both of them and said, "Thank you" softly, and we walked back into the tent. They were trying to be kind. They really were. But to a 12-year-old who just came to camp to be a normal 12-year-old, it felt like someone had just dug up a root of shame and embarrassment out of the ground and held it up for everyone to see.

I cried myself to sleep that night. I was absolutely humiliated. They had pulled me outside in front of everyone only to remind me that I was different. I knew it already, but they had pointed it out and then tried to tell me that they could relate when I knew they had no idea what it was like to wet your pants after three years old. The rest of the week flew by and was a lot of fun. I danced with a boy that wasn't my dad for the first time ever and walked away understanding what it felt like to be around a group of people who were sold out for Jesus at 12 years old. But even after all of that, one conversation pounded in my ear. *"I'm different,"* it said. I came here to be another camper, but they found out and now they see me *differently.*

When I was 12, God was calling me to be different. But it wasn't at the altar call at camp or at a Bible study. It was standing outside of a cloth-covered teepee with two exhausted counselors. To me, it felt like the rudest awakening. To God, it was another hard, yet kind, revealing of Himself. When I think about it now, I think He just laughed and shrugged. I can hear Him saying, *"Okay Lauren. I'll make sure and have some confetti poppers go off in the background next time,"* with a twinkle in His eye.

But in that difference came shame. It wasn't polite enough to knock but carelessly began to infiltrate my heart. It built up invisible walls of isolation and unworthiness and began to convince me that I was worth nothing because I had a problem at 12 years old that wasn't getting fixed.

I had a church leader in junior high that told me the same thing. "Be different," she would say. "You are called to be a light and be different." She would say it, and all the girls in our small circle would smile and nod like it was something so profound. I was never convinced. Everyone said that, but no one meant it. Being different than everyone else seemed like a great idea until you were *actually* different from everyone else and people treated you like it.

In 8th grade, I stopped showing up to my Sunday school class and started teaching kindergarteners instead. My leader, who happened to sit a few rows in front of my family every Sunday, noticed I wasn't coming and approached me, her hands rested slightly above her hips. I feel like this posture says a lot about our relationship.

Most of the Sundays I sat in that Sunday school class I heard all the disapproving things. I never felt like I fit in. I never felt I was good enough for her or the other people in the room. It felt like a finger in my face every time she spoke to me. I did not like her. Despite my weekly attempt to avoid her, she spotted me booking it down the stairs to my class one morning. "Where are you going?" she demanded. Avoiding eye contact, hands grasped tightly together behind my back, I told her the truth she didn't want to hear. "I'm not coming to class anymore. I teach kindergarten now," I whispered.

Her facial expression said it all and the words that followed were not ones of encouragement: "You're making the wrong decision. I can't believe you would do that." Because she had taught Sunday school for many years, she insisted the best place for me was in her class. Sunday after Sunday, she would catch me in the foyer again and berate me for leaving her group and teaching kindergarten. The people in my life who had told me I was "called" to be different were the ones yelling at me when I was.

Maya Angelou said it best: "I've learned that people will forget what you said, people will forget what you did, but they will never forget how you made them feel." I don't exactly remember what else that teacher said to me every Sunday when I ran into her in the church foyer. I don't remember what she was wearing, where she was going, or the exact words that came out of her mouth. But I will never forget the way she made me feel.

During my sophomore year of high school, my school's basketball team went to the playoffs. One of my best friends that year was a senior, and we drove together. I had never felt so cool arriving to a game with a senior. After buying our tickets, we found a spot right on the very last row of the student section. I was excited—tensions were high and the stands were packed with people. I sat down next to my friend but was immediately prompted by the senior guys leading the student section to get up for the player introductions. As our players were announced, we went crazy. But, as the opposing team's names were introduced, several senior guys started signaling and yelling to the student section to turn our backs to their team. I had thought the student section in the past had sat down and stayed silent. But turning our backs as a Christian school? I knew absolutely nothing about basketball, but I knew that wasn't right.

I stood, frozen, as students began to turn around and face me. More than 100 pairs of eyes stared right at me, and my face turned bright red. The senior class chaplain saw I was the only student who hadn't turned around and yelled at me by name from the very front row: "Just do it, Lauren. You're a part of the student section!"

I watched in horror as my friends beside me turned their backs without even giving it a second thought. I turned to my right to look at Kelsey, my senior friend who had graciously driven me and was a role model to me, thinking "Surely. Surely Kelsey will stand with me. Surely Kelsey will stand with me." Instead, she nudged me and whispered, "Lauren, just turn around. Just do it. Everyone is staring at you. It'll be over in just a second." The next 120 seconds were the longest of my life.

After the first quarter of the game, I turned around to see who was sitting behind me. It was the Cooper family, who had been family friends since I started walking. As I reached over for a hug, Mrs. Cooper looked me in the eyes and said, "Lauren, I am so proud of you. That took courage."

People are always watching. Just sometimes it's a hundred people and sometimes it's one. You have to be the one to start the movement, even if no one else follows. Character is what you do when no one is watching, but it's also what you do when everyone is watching.

Throughout high school, I tried to compensate for the things that made me feel like I didn't fit in. (Unless they were applauded, and then I boasted in them.) If I weren't perfect at something, I had to fix it by becoming good at something else. And that root only grew deeper and deeper into high school. I didn't make the varsity volleyball team, *but* I was class president. I didn't score high on the ACT, *but* I was a nationally recognized scholarship recipient. I lost the class president election senior year, *but* I was Key Club Vice President.

I was okay with being different when people nodded their heads in approval. But when approval dies, shame surfaces through the cracks. The root of shame that flourished on a wooden platform in front of a shaggy teepee at camp kept digging, digging, digging even deeper. Slowly, it was trying to grab me and pull me under. That's the thing with weeds: we can either let them fester and ruin the entire garden or pull them out. Hiding in the darkness is easy, but what happens when the sun comes out? Weeds can either slowly destroy you or help you see the parts of your life that need to come out of the ground.

I needed to be okay with me, whether I got the applause or a blank stare.

. . .

Years after that night in the student section, my roommate and I decided to join the same business organization (we were both business majors). Under the guise of needing something to throw on our resumes, I think we both hoped it would bring us a few friends.

One night, Sydney and I were in our dorm getting dressed up for the organization's monthly professional event. Pushing clothes out of the way, I picked up my nude heels hidden in the back of our 5x5 closet and gently blew the dust covering the tops. I hoped I would have worn them by now. Maybe to a dance, on a date…my mind continued to wonder. *Snap out of it, Lauren.*

"Hey Lauren, you ready?" Sydney asked from behind the curtain that covered our closet.

"Yeah, let's go!"

Phones in hand and purses at our sides, two pairs of clicking heels stepped out into the hallway, and the door slammed shut behind us. The 10-minute walk to the business building was quiet. Sydney and I were just happy to fulfill a requirement for the month.

We picked up a thin, white pamphlet on the way in, found two seats on the left side of the stage a couple rows from the front, and sat down in the large, acoustic auditorium. There were six barstool chairs on stage. I glanced down at the pamphlet in my right hand and saw the organization was hosting an internship panel with five seniors.

Our president, a beautiful, curly-haired senior, said a brief welcome and called the meeting to order. I leaned back into my cloth seat and crossed my legs, mentally preparing for them to be numb by the end of the meeting. It was going to be a while. As our president began to pass around the microphone and ask questions, each woman introduced themselves and spoke about the faraway places they had travelled and interned for. With every word they spoke, my heart started to beat faster and faster until eventually I was sick to my stomach.

My mind flashed back to the moment most college students would consider their very first moment of freedom: when their parents drove away.

"I didn't come here to be different again," I had whispered to myself as I watched my parents drive away into the sunset on I-35, leaving me with a tear-stained face in my dorm room. This was home now, but it didn't feel like it.

I'm learning now that home can be anywhere—it's the people that make it that way. Being in a new place is like building a new home. It takes time to gather the materials to put the structure together. Then you have to find that comfy couch to put your feet on, under a warm blanket.

It just takes time to find your people and make the new place feel like home.

My "welcome group" leaders, as they were called, had knocked on my door early that morning as I was hanging a bulletin board on the plain beige wall and left me a calendar of activities our group was going to do that night. Now, hours later, I was sitting on my bed holding the colorful card between my fingers. All I knew was that the faces on the card looked happy, and I did not. I could hear the trickle of rain falling and booms of thunder from my room and I wondered if the activities were canceled. I wanted to get out. Do something. I got up from my new bed and headed down the stairway, feet thundering in rhythm with the booms outside the building. When I reached downstairs, I approached the brown-haired student sitting behind the front desk. I figured he would be able to answer my question.

"Hi. Could you tell me if the welcome week activities are canceled? Is it okay to go outside?" I asked as weather sirens blared in the background.

He looked up from the computer and made eye contact with me. "I'm not your mom. You can do whatever you want," he answered matter-of-factly and then turned back to his work.

And that was when I knew. Even then, I had a choice to make. I could be like everyone else, or I could be Lauren Kinney and run outside anyway when it seemed unsafe and scary and different. This really wasn't about the weather. It was about what was going on inside of me as I was trying to figure out my place in this new place. Did I have to belong to be loved?

I know now I didn't have to belong to be loved. I just didn't realize how okay that was.

I snapped out of my daydream and turned my attention back to the five women answering questions on stage. Staring back at me sat future versions of myself. *This will be me in three years,* I thought. *But if this is what it looks like, then I don't want to be a part of it.*

It seemed stiff and formal, almost impersonal. I tend to be highly relational and prefer jeans and Birkenstocks over a dress and heels. Though I couldn't quite put my finger on it, I just knew it wasn't a place where I wanted to be. Right there, in an auditorium full of women who were made to wear business pants, I decided I wasn't one of them.

I realize now I wasn't ready. I was still trying to get used to living in Waco. I didn't like being told I needed to apply for internships across the world. The fear I thought I had so expertly stuffed deep down inside was now resurfacing with every word spoken by the six women in front of me.

Then why am I here? Did I even want to be a business major? Did I want to be at Baylor? I had been so sure this was what I wanted to do. *Help!* my mind screamed. My legs shaking, I debated getting up out of my chair and walking out of the room. *But then where would I go?*

So I stayed put, trying my best to focus on the glorious sun setting through the glass windows.

CHAPTER 5

HOW REAL ARE YOU WILLING TO BE?

It was the first question he asked me.

I was sitting in his office, fingers twitching excitedly when he walked in, admiring all the degrees and awards and pictures that hung on the white walls. Often our conversations were about assignments or grades, but I always ended up staying an hour later talking about what was happening in my life. I enjoyed hearing his nuggets of wisdom particularly about writing. After all, he was, in my opinion, Baylor's best journalism professor.

I couldn't keep the words in any longer. They fell out of my mouth, and I made no effort to shove them back in. "Professor Parrish," I began. "I'm writing a book." He turned his swirly chair around and smiled at me. With a straight face, he looked me in the eye and asked me a question.

"Lauren, how real are you willing to be?"

• • •

One September night during my freshman year, I was sitting on the stained white rug in my dorm room telling myself I would be lonely forever because I couldn't find someone to go with me to a weekly worship night on campus called Vertical. I had texted eight different people and received eight polite no's, which only further entertained the idea I would indeed be an old dog lady alone forever. As I sat there in a puddle of pity, I heard Him speak.

"Lauren, go anyway."

I knew what God was saying. And I didn't want to go. But I stood up off the rug, grabbed a jacket and my keys, and walked across the street to the parking garage. Seven minutes later, I pulled into the well-lit parking lot of the Baylor track field, where Vertical met. Cars pulled up beside me, their doors opening and students piling out. I watched a group of girls skip together to the entrance and buried my head in tears and shame. It was never supposed to be this way—sitting in my car watching the world around me hold hands and laugh while I felt alone and afraid.

After brushing my hand across my face to wipe my tears, I got out of my car and began walking to the front entrance. Nearly 20 volunteers greeted me with the biggest smiles. They offered me high fives, and I smiled. Maybe I would be okay.

I made my way up the metal bleachers, looking for someone else who might be alone. I noticed a girl sitting higher on the right and asked if I could sit by her. She said yes, and I sat down (not directly next to her as I didn't want to freak her out), secretly hoping I was close enough for it to look like we had come together. Bugs were everywhere, and I gave up trying to pick them all out of my hair. It was an unusually cold night in Texas and I was shaking from the chill, but I didn't care.

Things were going great—I didn't *look* alone.

The band began to walk up on stage and just as the chorus to the first song began, I looked over next to me. The girl was gone. I wish I could say I owned it, and maybe from the outside it looked like I was completely fine sitting by myself. But on the inside, every ounce of confidence was disappearing, and I was losing it. I was sick of being invisible.

An hour later, the speaker prayed to end his sermon and reminded the audience it was church night and to make sure we checked out the churches that had set up booths outside. The bleachers rattled as students picked up their Bibles and flooded back down into the parking lot. I made my way down and found myself on the grass outside. The man on stage wasn't joking about the church booths outside—there were at least 10 lined up next to each other. I had a choice. I could take a hundred steps in front of me and get in my car and bury myself in shame, or I could take two steps towards the friendly looking people standing behind the church booths and be brave. Maybe they would see me.

Before I could make the choice, my feet took two courageous steps forward. It's funny how complicated we make bravery out to be. It looks far ahead in front of us, but sometimes we just need to take two steps forward. I walked up to the booth closest to me, and a girl wearing a red flannel and round glasses stepped out from behind the table.

"Hi! I'm Erin!" she said, extending her hand with a huge smile. I shook her hand and told her my name, trying to match her level of excitement. After talking for a while, I asked for her number and told her we should get coffee sometime. A week later, we did. And nearly every week afterwards.

In January, I came back to rush a sorority and ended up dropping out the first day. I had waited until after rush to figure out housing for next year, but after I dropped out unexpectedly, I didn't have many options.

Erin and I got coffee a few weeks later. We found two chairs nestled in a corner at the coffee shop right across the street from campus, Common Grounds. After leaning over in anticipation to hear about why I dropped out, she sat back in her chair and asked if I wanted to live with her. I shook my head in denial at the next words that came out of her mouth: "Lauren, I've wanted to ask you since September."

I remember walking out of Common Grounds that morning in tears, repeating over and over again, "God, thank you for letting me show up that night." I didn't do anything special besides obey God's voice. And now I live (literally) with a reminder that God doesn't abandon His children.

If you would have told me that chilly Monday night during the fall of my freshman year I was going to meet my roommate for the next three years, I would have laughed and thrown my snotty Starbucks napkin at you. In fact, on that September night sitting in those cold metal bleachers, if God would have offered me the option to press a big red button and fast forward to the next day, I would have done a handstand on it (and I can't even do a handstand). Now, I can't believe how much I would have missed out on.

The first question Erin asked me wasn't if I went to church. She asked what my name was. She didn't stand behind the booth, but stepped out right next to me. There wasn't a table with a bunch of information cards between us. She didn't see me as a project, but another person she could love. I walked to my car that night knowing one thing: Erin wanted to know me for who I really was.

Before living with each other, Erin and I met nearly every week for coffee. Now I go four days without seeing her, even though our rooms are five feet from each other. We're leading completely different lives, but I think we both know this: He never abandons His children.

Erin and I have three words we repeat daily to each other, either on the phone, in a text, over a voice recording, or in person when we walk out the door in the mornings. Our phrase is a code word and encouragement all in one: "BEST DAY EVER." When Erin and the guy she's had a crush on for a year finally started dating, she texted me, "BEST DAY EVER." When I failed a test two weeks ago, I texted her, "BEST DAY EVER."

That lonely, hopeless night at the track field seemed like a setup for the worst day ever. But it turned out to be the beginning of a friendship in which God has used Erin to disprove the lie I believed for the first few months of college: He had forgotten about me.

A year later, I was sitting at the same campus worship night inside a warm building filled with hundreds of students (very thankful we'd upgraded from the track field) and our director announced it was church night. He asked all the college pastors in attendance to come on stage so he could pray over them and their ministries. My eyes filled with tears as I thought back to that night of horrid loneliness, and I wondered how many students in the room showed up alone. As he prayed, I thanked God for their courage—because it takes guts to simply show up. Silently I began to pray once again that God would use this huge room of students to show them they're not alone.

Once again, I walked outside the doors of the chapel and found Erin, still wrapped in her red flannel outside in the cold, getting to know students looking for a church home. She isn't ever behind the church's table covered with pamphlets, but always stands right beside someone, fully engaging them in conversation and making sure no one is standing there by themselves. I watched from a few feet away and hoped they asked her to coffee too. But they can't take my roommate.

God delights when we say yes. And most of the time that means showing up and trusting Him.

There have been many times even this year that I've asked God if I could fast forward to the day after an important meeting or scary conversation or confrontation (or an accounting test if we're being real). But I think back to that cold, insect-filled night at the track field and I'm reminded that days that look hopeless can actually be the days when we get to watch God move. Just because the day looks terrible doesn't mean God stops showing up.

• • •

I recently volunteered at a high school girls' conference. During one of the sessions, I snuck through the doors and found a seat towards the back. As soon as I sat down and looked around the room filled with over a thousand girls, I realized how lonely I was. No one was sitting to my left or right and no one other than the volunteer who shared my photo booth had even attempted to ask my name. Even at the volunteer dinner a few hours later, I sat and ate in silence because no one at the table would look at me. An hour earlier, I had taken pictures of hundreds of girls, and now, not one adult would acknowledge my existence.

I didn't matter. It doesn't matter. I drove home that night and cried a lot. I didn't understand how I could be sitting with more than a thousand girls and still feel like the only one in the room. At that point, no amount of outside applause could make my inward rejection disappear.

Every part of me did not want to show up the next morning to volunteer. But then I remembered the chapter I had written about showing up. And I prayed. Because I knew that somewhere in that audience of a thousand girls had to be one who felt that broken and alone too. So for the rest of my drive home, I prayed for her. I prayed that God would show her she wasn't alone and I prayed she (and I) would have the courage to show up again the next morning.

As I tucked my hands underneath my pillow late that night, I heard Him say it: *"You matter to Me. It matters to Me."* The world will silently scream at you that you don't matter. People will ignore you, be unkind to you, see right past you, and forget your existence. But you matter. *To Him.* So I put on my volunteer t-shirt and showed up again early that morning—not because God had promised He would do anything, but because I trusted Him enough to walk in obedience anyway. After lunch, the founder of the gathering invited a panel of four high school girls to the stage. As they passed the microphone between them, the girls told stories of brokenness and God's redemption and fierce love. But one story caught my attention: "My older brother, who's my best friend, left for college this year, and I've felt loneliness like never before."

I looked up from my chair. "He goes to Baylor and I try

to visit him on the weekends," she continued. Instantly I knew that was why I showed up that morning. Two weeks later, that girl and I talked for two hours at my favorite coffee shop in Waco about loneliness.

For every time we decide to show up, there are 10 other times we get in the car only to cry more, never hit the gas pedal, and cave to fear. But only He is able to transform our fear into an invitation. An invitation to see more of who He is. An invitation to His heart and love for you. I think it starts with showing up.

• • •

Whenever we turn 14 in my family, my dad lets us pick a place inside the U.S., and he takes us. Hannah, who is much cooler than I, picked California since she wanted to learn to surf. Conner picked Florida, where he envisioned himself pulling a 30-pound bass out of the water. Dillon has yet to choose, but I'm betting he'll pick some crazy fishing spot too. I was the first to start this family tradition and picked New York. I wanted to see the city. It looked beautiful in *Elf* and *Home Alone*, so it had to be in real life too. Dad bought the plane tickets and suddenly I found myself on the runway in LaGuardia. We grabbed a cab to our hotel, dropped off our luggage, and headed to Times Square. It was beautiful. The lights, the colors, the bustling people bumping into you from all angles. This was New York. And it was magical.

The trip was going beautifully until the next morning. I realized I had started my period, and my excitement went from 100 to 0 real quick. My dad and I were shopping at H&M in the skirts section when I burst into tears.

"Lauren, what's wrong?" he asked.

"Nothing."

Then he *knew* something was up. I wasn't actually sad or angry, but I had no control over the tears dripping down my face. I was humiliated. How could I tell him about my womanly problems? He wouldn't get it. He probably wouldn't even know what a period was. He was a *man* after all. My attempt to communicate my feelings and explain the tears accidentally came out in the form of some sassy comments in which I said, "I don't even want to be here anymore. Can we just go home?" I wanted nothing to do with him or this trip or my cramping body.

My dad was heartbroken—so much so that he called my mom and told her the trip was going terribly and he was booking the next flight home to Dallas. I don't exactly remember what happened right after that, but we soon found ourselves in a small frozen yogurt shop in Times Square. It was so awkward. I wouldn't talk to him and kept pushing his questions away. I was refusing to tear down my teenage know-it-all wall. Finally, after taking a few small bites of the fro-yo melting in the pink cup in front of me, I gave up and told my dad I was terribly sorry and that I was on my period and that I didn't actually want to go home but all I wanted was a bottle of Advil.

All of a sudden, my dad burst into laughter.

"I was going to book us plane tickets *home!*" he said. "I called mom and told her we were coming home. Lauren, the purpose of this trip is simply to spend time with you. I want you to enjoy it. After all, you picked our destination! This is your trip—I'm just happy to be here with you." The whole conversation took less than 10 minutes.

Not all of life's problems can be solved with a bottle of Advil, but I'm learning that swallowing my pride and being truthful when it feels uncomfortable can be the first step in correcting a course.

Hours later, we were laughing that my meltdown had even happened. The rest of the trip was incredible. We ice skated in Rockefeller Center while Frank Sinatra's "You Make Me Feel So Young" played over the speaker. I held my dad's hand tightly and we pictured ourselves beside Will Ferrell and Zooey Deschanel. I thought I was a pretty good skater, but then my dad started passing me around the rink, and it was on.

A couple days later, we grabbed McDonald's for breakfast and were walking in the middle of Central Park when my dad and his egg McMuffin went flying into the air and he landed flat on his butt, breaking the ice on the sidewalk. I turned around, crying tears of laughter with my finger pointed at him, my other hand over my mouth. After laughing at him for a few more seconds, I figured I should at least try to help him up. I took a few steps forward and flew up into the air. This time it was my butt that broke the ice.

My dad and I refer back to that yogurt shop often because it was there where the entire trip changed. I spilled the truth, as embarrassing as it was at the time, and truth was spoken in return. My attitude took a sharp 180-degree turn, and my dad was able to understand my crazy emotions and why I responded the way I did. Most importantly, I got some Advil.

He was so patient with me. If I had been him, I think I would have told my child to suck it up and slap a smile on their face. But not my dad. He was seeking to understand, and after pushing him away, he pressed me harder, which made me even more mad. But after spilling my guts about my womanly issues, it wasn't awkward anymore and we started communicating.

One vulnerable conversation in a yogurt shop in Times Square changed the trajectory for our entire trip—just like one courageous conversation after a campus worship night changed the trajectory of my entire freshman year. Sometimes you just have to show up and speak truth.

• • •

During my freshman year at Baylor, I decided taking people to coffee would be my thing. I was lonely and needed friends. And if I desired friends, I had to get to know people first. I texted or called or asked anyone and everyone I could. Three times a week, you would find me sitting in a booth at Common Grounds with a drink in my hand getting to know someone. I loved it. I loved knowing people. I loved passing faces on the sidewalk that I had once sat across from. But that was the furthest it ever went. I knew nothing more about them than what they could squeeze into 60 minutes before leaving and moving onto the next thing. My contact list was growing longer, but my heart was growing lonelier.

The introduction date was easy. There were a lot of those. But there was only a handful of people willing to stick around, who wanted a relationship deeper than waving hello across campus. I wanted more. Nothing was happening. There was no substance to my conversations. I was tired of standing on the surface.

The first time Erin and I sat down at Common Grounds, I remember sitting across from her and making a conscious decision to be real. To be honest. She could do three things: listen, listen and speak, or listen and run. But being real was worth the risk. I was tired of pretending to be real on the surface but not revealing my loneliness.

Eventually we've got to make a choice and decide what's worth standing up for and who we'll become. We can't keep living double lives. Faith and unbelief don't exist in the same body. Sure, there are always two sides to one story. But people with two sides of character not only aren't trustworthy, but they're also fake versions of themselves.

So that day I made a choice to go all in. I laid my dirty cards out on the table and Erin chose to stay and love me anyway. Real is who we were meant to be all along.

• • •

My friend Maggie told me once that her dad used to take her and her sister to the public pool on Wednesday night for Family Swim Night.

"My dad would take us to the deep end, hold onto me, and

begin to sink," she said. "When I ran out of air, I would tap him and we would rise to the top. After a couple weeks, I was able to sink to the bottom on my own. Here's what I'm learning," Maggie continued. "I can't go deep without my Father."

A tree can't grow without digging its roots deep down into the soil beneath it. "Vulnerability begets vulnerability," Maggie says. It's uncomfortable. Awkward. Heavy. Overwhelming. But if we want to go deep, we have to be real. We have to go deep in our hearts to go deep with our Father and the people around us.

My mom says it best: "The greatest treasures are deeply hidden and worth the pursuit."

We're cutting off our ability to love people fully if we hide the parts we don't want them to see. I've played myself for a long time, believing I really was going deep by simply showing up. Showing up to church just to make a to-do list in my journal. Showing up to coffee expecting deep conversation when I wasn't even willing to meet my friend halfway. It isn't enough.

Showing up isn't the same as going deep. Driving to the pool is the first step, but learning how to swim is an entirely different thing. The truth is, I don't want to go deep. It's hard and scary and you can't pretend to be perfect.

I'm jumping in anyway. It's over my head. I've realized

I've played myself and stayed shallow. I'm tired of the kiddie pool when I came for the high dive.

I still take people to coffee, but now I skip all the safe, boring questions. I'm trying to do the same with Jesus. I'm done settling for the shallow water. I want to be fully immersed in who He is and who He's made me to be.

The people in my life I admire the most aren't the ones who are the best at having it all together. They are the ones honest about where they are and the questions they are asking. To them, the cost of rejection seemed small for the prize of being free.

All of the stories written in front of you are real. I cried a lot while writing them. I didn't want to include some of them. But every time I hesitated, I heard my professor's voice in my head.

"Lauren, how real are you willing to be?"

C'mon. Let's dive.

CHAPTER 6

KNOW MY NAME

It had been a month since I had driven back from Christmas break, lost as I had ever been. Walking to the white brick building that held hundreds of students every week who sat in their seats either completely engaged and awake or sleeping on their own shoulder was just another thing on the list that gave me somewhat of a purpose. Due dates and the lack of breakfast food in my mini-fridge were the only two things getting me up in the morning. Chapel, like everything else, had become another chore. I was numb to it all, but you would have never guessed. And that's exactly how I wanted it to be. But for some reason, I kept showing up anyway. *I want something real. Show me something real.*

As I walked to chapel that morning, it was cemented in my mind. My car driving up the slick I-35 bridge. The muted car stereo and the deafening silence. The dark sky tinted by the tiny glimmer of small stars. The trash bags of laundry scattered across the backseat. Going back was the last thing I wanted. "Anywhere but Waco," I whispered through tears as I sat up straight in my seat. "Jesus I am ready. I am ready to go home. This is not where I thought I would be. Drop the bridge. Collapse it. I'm ready to go home."

Five days earlier, I had dropped out of rush at Baylor. Rushing had never been at the forefront of my mind. The summer before, I decided to ask a few friends if they could see me in a sorority. They laughed, and I laughed with them *Maybe for somebody else,* I thought. But a month before the deadline, the thought kept reappearing, and God said *"Lauren, you have nothing to lose."*

He was right. Only $50 and a week. So I signed up.

I spent the last week of my Christmas break at my favorite local store hunting down the perfect shoes for my cocktail dress. I drove back to Waco, nervous but praying I would find the community of girls I had been searching for. In the freezing cold on the first morning of recruitment, my leader led our group of girls into a stairwell right behind the room that would host the first party of the day. It was my first-choice sorority. *My luck,* I thought. I remember walking through a tunnel of smiles too big for eight o'clock in the morning but silently praying God would make it clear if this was what He wanted for me.

Thirty minutes later, the first party of the day ended, and I knew. It wasn't that I didn't like the people. A lot of them were already my friends. But I felt empty. During my lunch break, I ran back to my dorm and called my mom in tears while trying to shove apple slices in my mouth in the five minutes I had. "Mom, I just have a feeling. This isn't for me."

"Lauren, Dad and I would both like you to stay until there's a clear no," she said.

After all eight parties and two sore, bleeding ankles, I signed the form to drop out and walked out of the building. Two hours later, with a box of warm kolaches in my hand as a peace offering, I showed up at my front door, running through my speech I had prepared on the drive home. "Mom and Dad, I'm so sorry. I know we spent money on my dress and shoes and this jewelry and I've wasted it. I'm so sorry. I tried. I really did. But I just know. I know this wasn't right for me. I'm so sorry." I felt like I was reenacting a modern version of the lost son parable.

With kind eyes and warm hugs, they welcomed me inside, and my mom repeated the one line that meant the most to me my freshman year: "This is still your home and you are always welcome here."

And now I was back on campus. As I hurriedly walked to chapel that February morning, I passed Jason on the sidewalk. He saw where I was going and yelled past me, "It's a good one!" Then I remembered. I had seen it on Twitter the day before. Bob Goff was speaking at Baylor chapel. I had known who Bob was, simply because of his book, *Love Does*. But I hadn't read it—you could barely get me to read my textbooks. I just knew he was incredible.

I sat staring up at him for a full 30 minutes, completely in awe of a man who exudes pure joy in everything he does and lives to show people how to love like Jesus. This man had the energy of a child in a candy store and was laughing so hard that even if his jokes weren't very funny, you laughed with him anyway. When I walked on stage to meet him, I extended my hand to shake his, and he immediately embraced me in a hug.

Is this real?

I had forgotten what joy felt like. The first six months at Baylor had sucked the joy out of every part of me, and I wanted to know what that felt like again. As I walked out of the aisle to swipe my ID, the guy standing next to me in line shook his head and said, "Man, that guy lives with no fear." I nodded. Bob wasn't just a comedy show. He wanted everyone in the audience that day to love Jesus with the same joy.

As I threw my backpack over my shoulder and walked to

class, I couldn't hide the smile on my face. Even the most boring history lecture couldn't put it out. In fact, I got into the sandwich line at the dining hall and wanted the woman to mess up my sandwich just so I could show her the kindness of Jesus.

I dragged my roommate and another friend to hear Bob speak again that night. Afterwards, the three of us stood in the long line that remained, waiting for him to sign the last three copies of *Love Does* in the city of Waco. (I'm not joking.) Our turn came, and I stepped forward to hand Bob my book. He gave me a hug and asked for my name.

"Lauren," I said with a smile, looking up into his kind eyes.

He reached down and took the Sharpie from my hand. After signing my book, Bob put the lid on my Sharpie and looked me in the eyes. "Lauren, I see joy in you."

What. The. Heck. I got goosebumps. I smiled and gave him a hug and thanked him so much for being at Baylor. I walked out of the room that night holding back tears. I was stuck in a pit of anxiety and loneliness, trying to get it together and plaster a smile on my face. Something that looked real. And I was failing miserably. Yet Bob Goff, of all people, had the guts to tell me he saw joy in me. I sat up in bed that night staring at the ceiling, trying to process what had happened two hours prior. Did he really say that to me?

God, what are you doing?

Sydney was asleep, so I whispered the words that came to my mouth.

"Hello, joy. I know we haven't seen each other in a while. I've missed you. A lot actually. But I saw you today, and I guess you saw me too. Let me reintroduce myself. I'm Lauren."

Bob didn't know me. He didn't know all the junk I had brought into that room that night. He didn't know my anxiety or loneliness. He didn't even know my name five minutes before we meet. He simply asked for my name, then told me who I was. And I'll never forget.

I think deep down, we all know who we are. And we know who we want to be. Most of us are just waiting for someone to tell us.

There's a line that I love from the movie *Wonder*. The main character, Auggie, is crying in his mom's lap after being bullied at school. Julia Roberts, who plays Augie's mom, holds him as he cries and says, "You are not ugly, Auggie." Auggie isn't comforted and replies, "You just have to say that because you're my mom." In response, she looks him straight in the eye and says, "Because I'm your mom it counts the most because I know you the most."[2]

I know God loves me. I know who He says that I am. But most of the time I find myself listening to hear it from any voice but His, when in reality, because it's from Him, it means the most.

. . .

The summer before my seventh-grade year, my childhood best friend Melody called and invited me to her youth group photo scavenger hunt. Over the phone, I reluctantly said yes, but I was scared. I knew no one. Wednesday night quickly arrived and Melody, her sisters, and I pulled into the parking lot. We got out of the car and I walked slowly behind Melody as she approached the gym where we were meeting. Out of nowhere, a man ran up to me, high-fived me, and asked my name. He was young, but his black hair had a few gray streaks. Half-scared and very confused, I mumbled, "I'm Lauren."

"Lauren! I'm David! We're so excited to have you! Thanks so much for coming tonight!"

I regained my quiet composure and caught up with Melody. "Who was that guy?" I exclaimed, out of breath.

"Oh! That's David, our youth pastor!" she said as she flashed me a smile.

Once inside the gym, all the students divided into groups by grade and gender and got into our assigned car. Our chauffeur for the evening was one of the girl's dads, who immediately took the time to shake my hand and know my name before I jumped into his minivan. I'm pretty sure the seventh-grade girls came in last place that night, but I was blown away at the no-strings-attached kindness everyone showed me. When our time taking pictures with random people's dogs and making human pyramids at the local park was over (oh, the things junior high girls will do to try to win a photo scavenger hunt!), our driver stopped at the front of the church gym and all the seventh-grade girls piled out. As I unbuckled out of the backseat, he turned around and smiled at me. "Lauren! I'm so glad you came tonight!" he exclaimed.

As I walked to the door and waved goodbye, the same gray-haired but oddly young man came up to me again and thanked me for coming. By name.

I got home that night and couldn't stop talking about one thing to my parents: the youth pastor. "He remembered my name," I kept saying. "I can't believe he remembered my name AND our driver even remembered my name! He was so kind to me!"

The youth pastor of the church and someone's dad whom I had never met before had actually asked for my name. And remembered it.

When the school year started, my parents gave me a choice. I could go to my church's youth group or I could go to Melody's church. At Melody's church, the junior high group met separately from the high schoolers—at Melody's house, where I spent many afternoons after school playing in her family ping pong tournaments and eating all the food my mom didn't allow in our house. But it wasn't ever the location that made me want to keep going back.

I came back because I remembered how David high-fived me that Wednesday night, and I figured the people in the youth group would be that way too. I remembered the people who made me feel known and loved, and who showed me kindness. And the brownies were good.

I kept going to my own church on Sundays until I graduated high school, and not once did my youth pastor ever ask me for my name. It wasn't that he was a terrible youth pastor. In fact, it wasn't that at all. He was a great teacher, and I had friends that loved him. But I wasn't looking for someone to teach me fancy theology and throw me a dictionary. I just wanted someone who would know my name.

I grew up in the church. I grew up around pastors and leaders and families who loved Jesus. But even in a place where I had gone for 18 years, I still longed for someone to know my name.

Ten years later, David's still one of my favorite people. He's not a youth pastor anymore but studying to be a lawyer and show kindness through justice. And I'm willing to bet he's got a few more gray hairs now.

· · ·

During my freshman year political science class, my professor made the announcement: We were going to play Battleship.

He began counting students off down the row and asked all the numbers to go in one corner of the room. The way we played Battleship had some tie to American Constitutional Development, but I wasn't paying much attention. My eyes floated across the room as I watched my professor go from group to group, learning each of his students' names and shaking their hands. After we were done playing and he was done socializing, I headed back to my seat. The plastic tin game sets rattled as he carried them to the front of the room and explained why we played the way we did. Then, my professor stepped forward from behind the podium.

He pointed at a girl sitting on the first row furthest from him. "Jamie." The girl smiled and nodded. He pointed at the man sitting next to her. "Ben." Another affirming nod. "Emily. Sarah. Nicole. Chris." Four more smiles and nods. He kept going. With every name he called, more students' eyes began widening, and jaws dropped.

"Hannah. Ashley. Greyson. Sam. Liz." One by one, my professor looked each student in the eyes and told them their name. All 89 of them.

When he came to the last person, a girl sitting in the upper right-hand corner of the room, he paused, and the room went silent. "Madalyn." And with that, he raised his fist to the ceiling and pumped it in the air and spun around. "Have a great weekend," he exclaimed.

My professor valued his students so much that he made the effort to know their names.

The people in my life who have taught me most about Jesus have been the ones who have done the same and learned my name. This sounds silly, but it's true. I don't think we can truly love people like Jesus unless we know their name too.

• • •

One month after Bob came to speak at Baylor, I found myself in downtown Nashville in a room full of world-changers and balloons and confetti poppers and big dreams. It was then I decided I was done trying to conform to a world that kept telling me who I was: I wanted to tell the world myself. God used specific people in that room to affirm who I was in Him and propelled me to start writing this book.

God uses people and things to speak to us that will get our attention. What makes you do a double-take probably won't get a second thought from me. We're not all the same, so He pursues each of our hearts differently. He has to get creative—and that's where we really begin to see Him and know that He loves us individually.

It's easy to become enthralled by the men and women in our lives who lead us well. Whether it's your parents, an author, a pastor, or a worship band, we often point the spotlight so heavily on them, and suddenly we're trying to be more like them than Jesus. I'm so thankful for the leaders in my life who have taken me by the shoulders and pointed me in the direction of the cross. But if we continue to idolize our leaders, Jesus will become numb—He'll just be another author of another book or a voice that can just as easily be drowned out.

Here's what I don't want you to miss. Sure, Bob was there. But it was always Jesus.

CHAPTER 7

GET OUT YOUR BOOGIE SHOES

Rejection is a funny thing. It slaps us in the face and saves us from bigger bruises at the same time.

It was a few days before the end of February, and Sydney and I were at Starbucks doing homework. We sat side by side on two barstools in front of a giant window overlooking the cars passing by on I-35. The door swung open and a woman with short, black hair stepped inside. As the door closed behind her, I watched her brown eyes sweep across the coffee shop looking for an empty seat. Upon seeing that all the chairs and tables were taken, she walked to an open table outside and threw her bag on the ground. I watched her out of the corner of my eye, as she was obviously frustrated at something as communicated by her facial expressions and actions while she sat and worked.

I looked back down at my laptop and continued typing. *"Go ask her if you can buy her a drink."* I shuddered.

No. Thank. You, I told the voice in my head. Who in their right mind approaches a stranger who is clearly angry and older and then asks if they can buy them a drink? Not this girl. *I'll pass on this one,* I told God.

Ten minutes passed and I was still staring at her. Her frustration hadn't ceased for a second, and now she was typing angrily on her laptop. I wanted to forget what was being asked of me. But it had been at least 10 minutes and I hadn't been able to shake the thought out of my head and get back to studying.

"Go ask her if you can buy her a drink." I decided the worst thing that could happen was rejection. She could tell me no. And I had to be okay with that. I got up and walked outside to her table, trying to hide my hands shaking in fear. "Excuse me, ma'am, but I couldn't help but notice you look a little sad or frustrated about something. Could I buy you a drink?"

Her face tilted up, and as she glared into my eyes, she said "Um, no I'm not. And if I wanted a drink, I would have gotten one." Now I was really shaking.

I don't even remember what I said in response. I smiled softly and walked back inside to my seat. It took everything in me not to react with a face or roll my eyes or look down at my phone as an escape. I was embarrassed and humiliated and I knew people were watching. I wanted to run and hide. But I went back to my seat at the window and went back to work.

I kept replaying her response over and over in my head. The approach. My question to her. Should I have worded it differently? Maybe I should have waited longer? It was like a slap in the face. It hurts to be rejected. Especially when it's completely out of your comfort zone and the Holy Spirit tells you to do it.

As I drove back to my dorm that afternoon, I realized it probably wasn't about the lady accepting my offer to buy her a drink. It was Jesus asking me to step out in faith. He wanted me to trust Him and walk in obedience. And with a whole lot of hesitation and fear and ignorance, I did. As I gripped my steering wheel and tears dripped down my face, I prayed the woman didn't see the fear written all over my face. I prayed that somehow she saw Jesus in me.

Jesus doesn't always turn moments of obedience like these to greatness. Sometimes amazing things happen. And sometimes we get rejected and walk away blaming ourselves, either wishing we hadn't acted at all or wondering what we did wrong. But we *have* to step out in obedience. We *have* to do it anyway. I've spent a lot of my life worrying that my encounters with people have to be perfect. But Jesus was never looking for perfection. Just action.

• • •

During the first week of my sophomore year, I wanted to have people over to stream a young adult church service I watched all summer on Tuesday nights. Part of me wanted to put it out on social media and invite anybody who wanted to come. But the more I thought about it, I knew the chances of anyone showing up were close to zero. *People are busy. I'm not cool. Nobody cares.* But as I sat in class, debating the pros and cons, I heard God say, *"You have nothing to lose, Lauren."* And that was code for yes.

So I did. I spent a solid 10 minutes curating the most artsy picture, including all the details, and saying I would have Blue Bell ice cream (because you can't turn down Blue Bell). I posted it on Instagram and waited for people to DM me for my address. Every five minutes I would flip my phone over and glance at the lit-up screen to see if anyone responded. No one did. *No worries though*, I thought. *I guess the people who are coming already know where I live.* At 7 that night, I sat nestled in between the two couch cushions and waited for the doorbell to ring. It never did.

I realized that night it wasn't about people coming. I think God just wanted to see if I would be bold enough to post something I knew would likely bring failure and choose to walk in obedience anyway.

The courageous thing you do now, even in fear of failure, God can use to create a spark for a massive fire. The people God did the most with never had the most money or fame. They just said yes. They trusted God enough to know He could use the little they brought to the table and use it however He wanted.

I don't think God asks us to do crazy things sometimes because He promises to complete them. I think sometimes He just wants to know if we trust Him enough to start.

• • •

Erin hates it when people pick out a word for their year. "I think it's cheesy. Just another resolution that people don't keep," she said one night as we sat in two orange chairs at Common Grounds. "Lauren, I swore I would never be one of those people. But this year, I have a word." She paused and took a sip of her coffee. "Foolish."

"No really," she said. "I've been so conscious about my image for a long time. I've let my fear of what people think of me dictate how well I love and obey Jesus. This year, I'm embracing crazy."

Erin's right. If the people around us don't think we're crazy, then I wonder if we're really living the foolish life. My favorite character in the Bible is a guy named David. David's the guy who famously knocked Goliath out with a small stone.[3] He's also the guy who was berated for dancing in front of a crowd. This story is one of my favorites because it has my favorite word in the entire Bible—undignified, which means "appearing foolish." David, in response to the criticism, replies, "I will celebrate before the Lord. I will become even more undignified than this, and I will be humiliated in my own eyes" (2 Samuel 6:21b-22).

During my freshman year, I lived in a dorm with community showers. As soon as you opened the door to the bathroom around 10 o'clock at night, music loud enough to shake the floor would be blasting out of one small shower. The unspoken rule was that whoever started playing music first got to keep her music on, and few souls were brave enough to blend their pop Taylor Swift with someone else's Thomas Rhett. For the first couple months, I refused to play my own music, even when no one else was showering. Then one night, I did. I turned down the volume low so only I could hear it, then slowly raised it. Frank Sinatra sang so loudly I smiled and shook at the same time. My most thrilling nights were the nights when I got in the shower and turned the volume all the way up. In fact, during my last night in the community shower I danced and sang and went crazy. You are special and set apart for something. Be brave enough to play your own music.

• • •

Back in September, a friend and I entered a competition to fund our dream of having a worship night at a popular tourist destination in Waco. People from all over the world come to visit Magnolia, the wildly successful market opened by a local couple.

The Sunday before we expected the results of the contest, I drove to the Silos late in the afternoon to pray. It was Sunday, so walkways normally flooded with people with Magnolia bags hanging on their arms and cupcake icing on their faces were empty. I noticed a small parking lot across from the entrance, glanced around for any police, and took a hard left turn to pull inside.

Even though the calendar read September, the stickiness and heat felt like July. I rolled down my windows and stared at the two silos. Music softly rang from my speakers, and I began to pray when I heard Him speak: *"Get out and worship, Lauren."*

I got out of my car and closed the door. My feet hit the concrete and the stale, hot air began blowing through my hair. *"Worship Me, Lauren."*

So there, on the concrete, right across from Magnolia, a girl with a long, brown ponytail obeyed. Hands lifted, tears streaming down my face and music shaking the concrete beneath my feet, I sang loud and danced. "All hail King Jesus," I sang.[4] *"Louder,"* He said.

My hand reached back into the car and swung the knob to the right. Max volume. And I danced outside on the hot pavement like no one was watching. I heard the squeaking of car tires and knew people were staring. I wanted so badly to open my eyes and see who was watching and the expressions on their faces, but I kept them closed. The beat beneath my feet ended, and I opened my eyes and smiled. This was what it felt like to be foolish. Undignified. It was crazy. And I liked it.

After meeting a friend for dinner, I went back to Magnolia to pray again. This time I walked directly in front of the black gates encircling the tourist destination. As the sun began to set and colors of pink, orange and yellow closed in, I pressed against the cold metal bars and reached up and slid a few of my right fingers through the small metal grates, leaving my hand clinging to the wall. I stood still for a few minutes and pictured what it would look like one day to show college students Jesus' crazy love for them at this place.

God, I don't know what you're going to do tomorrow. But whether or not we get it, thank you for being a God who loves when Your children have crazy dreams.

I heard footsteps behind me and turned around. Two women stood a few feet from my left, admiring the sunset and peering into the marketplace behind the metal gates. One looked to be in her mid 20s. Tattoos covered her arms, and I knew instantly she had a story worth telling. The other woman, who was posing for a picture in front of the bold-lettered Magnolia sign, had to be her mom.

"Mom, move over to the left more. I'm trying to get the whole sign in the picture."

"Alright, alright. How do I look?" she asked, adjusting her hair.

My dad has taught me a lot of things in life, but at the top of the list is this: if someone is taking a picture of their friends or family, always ask if you can take one with all of them in it.

I took a few steps towards them. "Do y'all want one with both of you guys in it?" They turned around.

"Yes!" they echoed in unison. "Thank you so much!"

The younger woman handed me her phone and I snapped a few pictures. "Lauren," I said as I extended a hand. "Liv," the younger one said. "This is my mom, Cheryl."

"So nice to meet you guys! Where are y'all from?"

"Kentucky," Liz answered. "We were just in San Antonio meeting up with friends and now we're headed back home tonight. Figured we would stop here before driving through the night."

"So what are you doing here?" Liz asked.

For a moment I thought about cutting the story short and just saying I enjoyed viewing the sunset at the silos or was out on a walk. But I didn't think God told me to go back to Magnolia after dinner that night just so I could snap a picture of two women from Kentucky and not tell them why I was actually there. So I told them. Everything. About the dream, about our video entry for the contest, and how it felt crazy, yet we were jumping in anyway. I turned back to look at the gate and pointed to the stage. "I just want people to know how much God loves them."

They think I'm crazy, I thought. *Maybe I should have stuck to the sunset story.* I looked up at Cheryl and Liz, expecting them to give me puzzled looks with furrowed brows. Instead, they smiled at me. "Wow," Liz said. "I wish I were as crazy as you."

The sunset was well over, and it was beginning to get dark.

Before Liz and her mom climbed back into their Dodge Durango, we prayed together. As they drove away, I crossed the sidewalk to the parking lot and unlocked my car. The two golden silos grew smaller and smaller in my rearview mirror as I headed home, and I smiled again. I thought back to that time at Starbucks when I had been totally rejected and felt crazy. Now, I still felt foolish. But it was different this time.

I think the more you practice brave, the more confident you can be when you feel foolish.

A friend once showed me a video he took at a mall a couple of years ago. A young man in his 20s had set up a table with a stereo and two large speakers. As the music began to play, an older man in his mid-60s started to dance, *in the middle of the mall*. This wasn't your average mild dancing that's more like awkwardly swaying back and forth with the occasional foot tap. This man was full-on dancing—by himself.

The solo dance went on for a couple of minutes until another woman joined in and they started to dance together. Countless people walked by and smiled, laughed, or completely ignored the dancing altogether. I wish I could say this video ended with a massive dance party in which everyone who watched joined in, but it was just the man and woman brave enough to boogie while the rest of the world looked on.

Most of the time we think the world watches with judgmental eyes, but I wonder how many of those who walked by thought, *I wish I were brave enough to dance like that.*

There is a big difference between having the courage to be crazy and living an undignified life. I've watched this video more than a few times because it always reminds me how brave and bold we have to be to be different.

Since I was a little girl, my dad and I have always loved to dance. We've two-stepped and twirled and dipped in the craziest of places, including two World Series, ice skating in Rockefeller Center during New Year's, our favorite concert venue in Dallas, and my favorite spot—our living room. But for every time my dad has reached out his hand to me and offered a dance and I smiled and took it, there's been a time when I pushed back his hand and shook my head and mouthed, "Not now, Dad." But I will tell you, my biggest regrets in life have been not dancing with him when he so willingly wanted to dance with me.

I'm not trying to be crazier like Erin this year or dance like the old man in the mall. I'm trying to be more like Jesus and the best version of Lauren Kinney living an undignified life.

We have to decide if a lifetime of embarrassment is worth an eternity with Jesus. This is why. This is why we choose to do the hard thing, even when there's a forecast of fear and a chance of rejection. Loving Jesus doesn't equate to living comfortably.

Get out your boogie shoes. And don't stop dancing.

CHAPTER 8

FEAR STOPS AT THE GATE

I didn't really want to answer the phone. I sat in the left side of the small wooden seats inside Waco Hall, listening to the man on stage preach. My Bible in my lap and pen and journal in hand, I was looking for anything but an interruption. My head was spinning with 20 billion thoughts and I hoped every word booming through the speakers would mute them out.

Twenty-four hours earlier, I was in Atlanta with a friend taking the next step in pursuing a crazy dream to creatively serve college students through a worship concert. Instead, the trip had been a total bust. Flying back to Dallas late that night, I sat in my aisle seat with fear and frustration boiling in my stomach.

Meetings had fallen through and we had missed the exact reason we had flown up to Atlanta in the first place. Everything that could have gone wrong did. We had missed it. And I'll never forget that feeling. "It was never supposed to be this way," I whispered to myself as the plane gently touched down on the runway.

Back to that wooden seat with the swirling thoughts I was attempting to suppress. My watch started to vibrate on my wrist and I knew who was calling. I grabbed my phone underneath my seat and watched it shake in my hand. The sermon was still wrapping up. Surely this could wait.

It couldn't. I jumped out of my seat and walked up the carpet aisle, head down like it would suddenly make me invisible to the 1,000 pairs of eyes staring back at me. I stepped outside, my phone still buzzing in my right hand, and stopped before I reached the street. The buzzing stopped. I unlocked it quickly and dialed again. Phil answered.

I thought back to when Phil and I first met in Nashville at a conference. He sat at the front of the room. I'm not surprised now that I've gotten to know him. Phil has a way of making every person feel like his best friend. Phil cheers loudly for me and encourages me to hold nothing back.

I began to unpack the past 24 hours in a riveting five minutes. The other end of the line was silent as I went on and on about how disappointed I was and how God had opened a door, then slammed it right back in my face.

"Phil," I said. "What do I do now?"

Phil paused before his voice rang into my speaker. "Lauren," he answered. "Sometimes we have to see the things right in front of us to see the things God has in store for us. Don't miss out on any opportunity right in front of you."

Since I stood outside on that August night and listened to Phil's wisdom, I've tried to live it out, but honestly, I think I've spent more time engaging with my computer screen than with the people in line beside me at Starbucks. We're praying for purposeful encounters but we're missing them. We're distracted by everything else except the One who is begging for our attention. And we don't even realize it.

Sometimes I ask God for crazy things. And I think He loves for us to ask. But most of the time, I think He just wants to know if I'll love the person right in front of me. Jesus could be right in front of you and you're missing Him.

Please don't miss it.

• • •

Five days after I called Phil, I found myself driving to Ft. Worth to see him and his wife, Gina, who happened to be near my hometown for a wedding. The drive up gave me a lot of time to think about the week, and I still wasn't done processing it all. The trip to Atlanta had been a bust, my accounting class was already kicking my butt, and I was officially living with Erin. Everything was new and yet everything was the same. I pulled into the parking garage across from their hotel and grabbed a tube of Chapstick from one of the cluttered cupholders filled with coins, hair ties, parking stubs, and receipts that were pieces of memories I didn't want to get rid of. I pulled down the mirror and saw her. There she was, hair straightened and mascara on. She looked put together, but she knew better. She was so lost.

I walked through two large glass doors held by bellboys with polished shoes in black suits and texted Phil I was in the lobby. I sat down on a nearby couch. I was going over my mental outline of events to share with Phil and Gina when someone said my name. I looked up to see both of them walking out of the elevator towards me. I stood up and adjusted my kimono and hugged them. A few minutes later, we were standing in their hotel room.

There were no walls. Instead, only windows framed the room. Sunlight flooded in, creating shadows that danced whenever you moved. "The hotel just opened right when we got here. We were the first guests," Phil said, pointing to a basket of fruit and cheese sitting on the gleaming granite countertop. I walked up to one of the windows and put my hand on the glass. All of Ft. Worth stared back at me. For a second the room went silent and only the city was unmuted. The cars honking below me, passersby walking back to their cars from work, the smoke rising from the rooftops. It was beautiful. Standing above the city, I felt invincible. Capable. Strong. The frustration from the week melted away and for a few seconds I forgot Phil and Gina were even in the room. It was just me, surrounded by a city that had become a part of me. I had become a part of it. I kept my hand on the glass, as if at the touch of my fingertip the glass would shatter and all of Fort Worth would become my playground and I would feel free. But I knew it wouldn't break. And I felt stuck.

Phil and Gina sat down on the couch and I picked a chair across from them. I didn't expect much from our conversation that afternoon. After all, Gina and I had just met, and I figured we would spend the hour letting her get to know me and catching up on the past five months. Phil asked me to tell Gina about my dream to write a book and words began fumbling out of my mouth as conversation continued. There was a pause, and Phil looked at me.

"I was talking with someone the other day and he asked me, 'What is the most negative emotion you're feeling right now?'"

I knew what was coming and I wanted no part. *Gina and I just met, Phil. Really?* But I should have known from the beginning I was there for more than small talk. "Lauren, what's the most negative emotion you're feeling right now?" Phil asked. I froze. Phil's icebreaker questions are more like therapy sessions, and that was the last thing I wanted.

"Anxiety. Before coming to Baylor, I struggled badly. I was afraid of trading a familiar place I loved with fear of the unknown. It's definitely not as bad as it was then, but it exists," I answered. Suddenly, in an instant, I felt as if someone had just ripped all the layers of my skin off me. Not gently peeled layer by layer, but all at once. It was as if I were left standing bare and raw in front of people whose trust I was trying to gain. I wanted them to like me. To see me as brave and kind and just real enough without revealing my brokenness.

For the next hour and a half, Phil and Gina prayed over me and I sat there in the soft, velvet chair with my eyes closed trying to process what the heck I was doing in a hotel room in downtown Ft. Worth on a Friday.

At one point while we were praying, I could see myself in downtown New York, where I had just been the month before. I was standing on the corner of Lower Manhattan and Greenwich St. in a glass box, just in front of the building that contains my favorite market, Eataly. Women with high heels, men with briefcases, and children holding their parents' hands kept walking by me in every direction, but to them, I was completely invisible. My sore arms kept banging on the box, screaming, "Let me out!" I remember feeling so frustrated that everyone besides me was fulfilling their purpose, and I was stuck in this glass box watching everyone else living out their own story. I knew my potential. I knew I was born to do great things. But I couldn't get out and prove it. I was stuck.

The New York City skyline faded away and now I was sitting on a wooden bench in the most beautiful garden surrounded by a gate. Flowers and trees grew around me. A man with the kindest eyes and softest smile I'd ever seen came and sat next to me. Slowly, He put His arm around me and I felt safe. I leaned in and looked up at His face and He smiled. We said nothing. I wasn't looking for an answer. I just wanted someone who would be present. Who would see me. Who would love me.

What was revealed to me as I sat with Jesus wasn't what I thought I needed. For the first time in a long time, I wasn't looking for an arrow in the sky or a new roadmap or another piece of advice to get to where I wanted to go. I just wanted someone who could be with me while I was confused and lost. Jesus didn't say anything to me because He knew it wasn't what I needed.

So often in our moments of desperation and loneliness what we really need is a friend who will sit with us and hold our hand and listen to us cry. Once we realize we actually are lost, instead of getting out of the pit, we want someone who will climb in with us. We feel safer when we're with someone. That sunny afternoon in Ft. Worth, Phil and Gina climbed down in the pit with me.

I felt even more confused and lost walking across the street back to my car. But something had changed. Now, I knew I had someone who would sit me with me on a bench in a garden. Sometimes no words say everything.

As my car drove back down I-35 that night, I repeated five words over and over again.

"Fear stops at the gate."

The walls around my heart were cracking. Breaking. Close to ruin. But Phil's question shot an arrow in just the right spot, and they came crumbling down.

Behind the walls was pain. Pain built up over the past year. Lingering anger behind the wall. Dead weeds that had accumulated over the past year for every time I asked God, "Where are you?" and didn't hear an answer. It was ugly and too ugly for anyone else to see.

And yet Jesus walked through the gate anyway and saw a garden. He saw a garden. And when I looked behind the wall, I saw a garden. The most beautiful garden.

Lauren, fear stops at the gate.

I got out of my car and walked up to my apartment building. My right hand reached up to type in the code to open the gate encircling the four apartments.

I took a step back and froze.

Fear stops at the gate.

"Well, crap," I blurted out loud standing in the dark on the concrete. "And it's only the first week of school."

• • •

Three months flew by, and it was November. School was no joke, I was working 25-hour weeks, and the only time I could find to write was early in the morning before my classes. I was tired and frustrated that the thing taking most of my time was what I was least passionate about: school. I was trying my hardest to be present, but my advisor didn't want to hear about the book I was writing. The only thing he was even remotely interested in talking about was my "four-year plan." I would sit in his office, take a deep breath, and for 30 minutes act like I knew what I was doing with my life.

I didn't know how to tell him that I couldn't even decide what to eat for lunch later that day, much less figure out what the heck I was going to do the next three years. I was spending hours studying for a class I was failing and it all seemed pointless. Instead of rewriting formulas and financial statements in high hopes they would stick in my brain, I wanted to be writing or taking someone to coffee. Accounting only made me feel dead inside, but I was dying to come alive. I wanted to do something with an eternal value, and school wasn't it.

One afternoon, I was sitting across from a friend at Common Grounds, holding a Styrofoam cup of water with lemon from Chick-fil-A in my right hand (pretty sure that goes against all rules of coffee etiquette).

"Lauren," my friend began. "Yesterday I was talking to a friend and we were having an incredible conversation. You know, one of those where you feel your purpose coming alive. I had class at the time, but this was much more important."

After waving at the group of dogs behind us, he paused and leaned back in the wooden chair that sat directly across from me. "Lauren." He stopped again. "I skipped a midterm."

My eyes got ten times wider and I let out a gasp while trying to contain my laughter. He continued: "My professor ended up letting me re-take it and I'm so thankful for grace I don't deserve. But that conversation was worth more than a political science class ever will." He sat up. "Why am I wasting time doing political science homework that has no eternal value?"

If it wouldn't have caused mass confusion and the gravel backyard had been completely empty, I would have jumped up out of my chair and run circles around the rocky backyard. *"YOU GET IT! FINALLY! SOMEONE GETS IT!"* I wanted to scream.

But instead I sat back in my wooden chair, lips pursed around my plastic straw, sipping my water like it was completely normal to skip a college midterm for a conversation. I shook my head and smiled. I'm not crazy. What my friend didn't know was that he had just repeated verbatim what I'd been voicing to my parents and roommate since March. I think deep down a lot of us are wondering the same thing. Why am I here? What am I doing? Does my life have any value? Do I or my work matter? All of this. Why do we do it if it's not eternal?

I've had this conversation too many times this semester. But the more I talk to people, the more I realize I'm not the only one desperately trying to figure out why the paper due tonight and accounting test tomorrow mean anything.

A friend and I wrote letters back and forth during my sophomore year. He was a freshman at Notre Dame at the time. I always wrote him with my best advice and he never failed to suppress my wisdom with humor and sass, which made him the best pen pal. Just when I thought I knew everything, he would say something really profound and it would catch me off-guard. I opened my mailbox to a letter from him one day. "To the queen herself" he had written above my name and address. In my letter to him that had arrived days before in the freezing temperatures of Indiana, I had complained about the uselessness of my schoolwork and how there was no joy in it. "This was never what I pictured," I had written in blue ink. "I keep hoping I'll come alive in it and I'm not."

Back in my bedroom, I held his letter and read down to the very last sentence, shoved in the far right-hand corner of the paper since he had run out of room. "Lauren, no one comes alive doing schoolwork. But this degree is a building block, and you need to finish it." His words felt like a punch in the gut, but I knew he was right.

I asked my friend Ellie once what she does when she gets discouraged by school and her purpose. "Well, Lauren," she began. "My mission and role in life right now is to be a student. And I have to do well in school in order to complete what Jesus has called me to do, which right now is to go to medical school and become a doctor. I ask myself a lot 'Is it even worth it?' But the answer is always yes, because my intentions are for eternity."

• • •

I've spent the past 20 years of my life looking forward to the next person, place, thing. The next day, week, month, year. Always wanting to get there faster. I wanted to skip the braces stage of junior high, then the SAT in high school, and fast forward to graduation. In college, I was ready to turn my tassel and be done with that chapter, too.

College is four of the craziest, most beautiful, terrible and transformative years of one's life. It is four years of training to move on to real life. Ha! Adulting. So how do we *be* here in a world telling us where we need to go and what we need to do? What if we've spent our entire lives waiting and preparing when God wants to us keep moving? And if we keep waiting, what do we keep missing?

We keep waiting for the right place and the right time. We need to get over ourselves. We're not here forever on this earth. If we keep waiting and waiting, then we'll never do it. We've tricked ourselves into this illusion that the time has to be "right." We keep waiting for the right moment, the right day, the right mindset: the perfect conditions. The reality is that the time will never be perfect. So, the perfect time is now. God asks us to wait sometimes, but sometimes I've used that as an excuse not to move when He says to move. But I often forget that I'm not in the present so that I can live in the future. I'm here, right now. So what am I doing to make sure I'm not constantly waiting but seeking God's will for me *right now?*

I'm making my move.

• • •

I'm a dreamer. I have a lot of them: that people would know Jesus. That we would shatter the glass walls we feel trapped in. That God would use my words. In book form.

That one day a band would stand on stage at Magnolia and sing of Jesus' radical love for college students. That people would know the depths to which they're loved. That we would trade loneliness for loveliness and hurt for healing. That worship would reside outside of the church's walls.

To see beauty in brokenness. To know fear would stop at the gate. To have courage to dance in the rain. To love so crazy big that people would see a difference maker. To have confidence that chaos would result in clarity and pain would seek promise. To pursue people with a love so reckless and wild that they want to know the source.

That we would move from seeing the things right in front

of us to seeing the things God has for us. That people would want to know where my dreams come from.

Rather, Who my dreams come from.

But we weren't made to fall in love with our passions or purpose. We were made to fall in love with Jesus. Our passions and purpose are just part of who Jesus made us to be. My dreams are big. But so is He.

We don't follow the dream. We follow the dream-maker. Because He is the God who holds them and cherishes them and hands them to us so that together we may see them through—hand-in-hand—*together*.

Starting right where we are. It won't be wasted time.

CHAPTER 9

CONFETTI POPPERS
AND CAKE POPS

My seventh-grade science teacher was one of those teachers who wrote on the white board in permanent marker. I remember my biology class gasping in horror as she picked up a black Sharpie and started to draw the phases of an amoeba on the whiteboard. She finally realized her writing wouldn't erase and started laughing hysterically. The silence broke and suddenly the entire class was laughing with her, and together we traced the Sharpie lines with dry erase markers and wiped the board clean. Mrs. Henry was also the teacher who enthusiastically exclaimed, "The radio must have been turned on!" whenever my friend's phone rang in class one day and made us do fingers exercises and sing biology life cycle songs with her.

Mrs. Henry was the most joyful and energetic teacher I've ever had. Back in 7th grade, I loved her, but also thought she was just oblivious and kind of odd. I mean, she made us sing songs about the life cycle of an animal. As I look back now, Mrs. Henry was weird compared to my other teachers because she didn't just want us to pass her tests. She wanted each of her students to know that they were loved and known.

I remember Mrs. Henry for two reasons: her loud laugh and always having a Diet Coke in her hand. It didn't matter if you were the star athlete on the junior high football team or the kid in the back who slept the entire class. When you walked in the door, Mrs. Henry would raise her Coke to you. Because in her eyes, you were always worthy of celebration.

I think God feels the same way about us. Even in our biggest mess-ups and total failures or when we write in permanent marker on a dry erase board, He doesn't shield His eyes in horror. He's gently whispering, *"Hey, you're still worth celebrating."*

When I was in high school, I'd stop by Mrs. Henry's classroom often. And every time, without fail, she would stop what she was doing and raise her Coke to me. Mrs. Henry didn't just acknowledge my presence. She acknowledged who I was. So many of us know who we are. We're just waiting for someone to tell us. I find this to be true all the time. We can only listen to ourselves for so long before our voice gives out and we stop talking. Or God starts shaking His head and slowly whispers into our hearts so that His word begins to intersect with ours. And soon enough, His words are left standing alone. Like permanent marker on a dry erase board.

• • •

During the summer after my freshman year at Baylor, I nannied full-time and took nine hours of classes. Most of my friends were working at camps across the country or traveling abroad and doing much more Instagram-worthy things with their lives. It seemed like everyone was out loving people in huge ways at camp or abroad. But all I was doing was babysitting, Business Calculus, and Microeconomics. The summer everyone dreams of, right?

I wanted something more, so I started asking God to give me a way to love people really big. A few days later, He told me to write all my contacts. He was specific too. No texts, but a handwritten letter to every person on my contact list. *"Tell them what I see in them, Lauren."*

I remember sitting down on my couch when He said that and scrolling down to the bottom of the list and looking at the number. *Shoot*, I thought. *That's a lot of stamps and notecards.*

But I had asked for something big, and clearly God had not held back. I said yes and ordered 500 notecards with my name in a cute font at the top and phone number, Instagram handle, and blog link at the bottom. Then I made an Excel spreadsheet with all the names of my contacts in alphabetical order. As I began typing up each name, I got super excited. *I'm doing it*, I thought. *Let's go.*

I hadn't even gotten through the "B"s when I saw her name. *Nope. No way.* I nearly closed my computer. *I am not writing her.*

I took a deep breath and remembered. *Say yes and don't worry about the next thing.*

I continued to the "C"s and was typing the "M"s when I realized I had the names and phone numbers of people I hadn't talked to in 7+ years. These were names I barely recognized and names I didn't want to recognize. These were people who had hurt me. I had no interest in writing letters to these people. How was I supposed to tell them I saw Jesus in them when I still couldn't shake the hurtful words they had spoken over me?

My initial excitement hadn't even lasted two minutes and I was already sitting in defeat. I heard Him again. *"Lauren, just tell them who I made them to be."*

A few days later, after a huge brown cardboard box showed up on my door step, I gathered all the colorful pens I could find and made my way to Starbucks. As I chewed on my green straw, I did the math. Ten cards a day meant I could get them all done in less than two months. I could do this.

So it began. I ripped open the first package of cards and grabbed a pen. Three hours later, I looked at my watch and set down my pen. I glanced to my right at the light blue envelopes. There were *eight*. Letters I assumed would be surface-level actually had me searching for more space to write after I had filled the entire front and back. I began pouring my heart out to people I had talked to maybe twice in my life. Suddenly it became way less about making the deadline than taking the time to speak words of truth over people. If it took me five years, I was still in.

I still haven't finished. And honestly, I don't care. Because truthfulness and vulnerability run a much longer and impactful race than rushed words.

When I was in 10th grade sitting in marine biology, one of my classmates gave me a letter from a senior girl I barely knew. When I got home that day, I opened the brown envelope and pulled out the small piece of paper inside. The entire card was covered in words. I had never seen smaller handwriting in my life. She went on and on about how loved I was by Jesus and how beautiful He sees me, and I sat on my hardwood floor in my room and cried. I barely knew her. How in the world did she know the words my heart desperately needed to hear? Over the span of 500 tiny, handwritten words, this high school senior told me who I was and that I was worth celebrating.

I am becoming convinced of one thing: we discover who we are when we celebrate other people.

I've learned a lot about myself writing these letters. Often the people I know the least are the ones to whom I write the most. This is funny to me, because there is much greater risk in writing to someone you barely know versus someone you talk with every week. But there is also something freeing about trusting someone you barely know. It's not that I trust the person—I trust the God who knows what to do with my words, and in Him I find the courage and freedom to write the truth that He speaks.

• • •

I came across a few names that shouldn't have been listed. Caitlyn's was one of them.

Caitlyn came to shadow me one day at school in 9th grade. I knew nothing about her beforehand, only that a girl my age was interested in coming to my school. I was running late that day, probably because the Starbucks drive-thru had taken longer than I anticipated. Just as I shoved my Hawaiian flowered backpack on the book rack, I turned around to see the smiling admissions counselor and a girl with long, blonde hair extensions wearing more makeup than I had ever worn in my life staring back at me.

"Lauren, this is Caitlyn. She'll be shadowing you today." I finished shoving my book in my bag and stuck out my hand. "Hi, I'm Lauren." She sat next to me during English class and I watched her fingers fly across the screen of her iPhone as she texted her friends and scrolled through Instagram. I was beginning to get the feeling she wasn't interested in my school at all.

I never wanted her number in the first place. At lunch that afternoon, one of my friends pulled me aside in the auditorium and asked if I could get her number. "She's cute!" he said while I rolled my eyes. "Would you get her digits for me?" So I did. And that's how Caitlyn's number ended up in my phone.

When I texted Caitlyn for her address five years later, I was surprised she even responded. But she did. "Why?" she asked. And I feel that. Because if someone that I hadn't talked to in five years sent me a letter, I would definitely want to know why.

I froze when that notification popped up on my phone. I didn't know what to tell her. In all honesty, I had no interest in writing her. But I wrote the letter and mailed it.

If you're expecting a happy ending, I don't have one for you. She never responded. I don't even know if she got it. Or if she opened it. I can't control any of the latter. But I dropped it in the mailbox and told God He could do whatever He wanted with it. And sometimes, I think that's the best we can do.

• • •

School started back up and I was trying my best to write as many letters as I could, but I started getting bored. Blue envelopes were fun, but I wanted something that would make people want to have a dance party.

I know someone who sends people cake pops in the mail. I loved the idea and thought I would try it too. On my way home one afternoon, I went through the Starbucks drive-thru. I figured two would be a good start.

"Could I get two cake pops please?" I said. As I waited at the stoplight five minutes from my apartment, I reached into the paper bag and put one in my mouth.

That was when I knew—this wasn't going to work.

Realizing this story would most likely end with me eating 300 cake pops, I turned my car around and drove to the grocery store. Confetti poppers in the party aisle caught my eye, and I dumped every last one into my basket.

"You having a party?" the girl at the register asked me, with one eyebrow arched into the air. I could only laugh.

Now, instead of finding myself in the Starbucks drive-thru, on any given day you can find me perusing the party aisle at H-E-B.

The times in my life when I felt the most celebrated weren't on my birthday or when I passed a test. It was when unexpected people spontaneously reminded me I was worth celebrating. I didn't do anything to deserve their applause, and that was when I needed to be reminded the most.

My roommate delivers donuts during finals season. My mom mails stickers and chocolate chip cookies to my friends at college. I send people confetti poppers. There are a million ways to celebrate people. Pick one and do it. A lot.

We weren't made to be fortune tellers and tell people what they'll be. God wants us to tell people who they are, and that they are worth celebrating.

Speak words of life like confetti.

• • •

My senior year of high school, my parents decided I should meet with a career counselor. I wasn't exactly sure what that was or what they did, but we had a family friend who had met with this lady, and she had helped him discover what he wanted to do with his life. Figuring out what I wanted to do with my life sounded great to me, so I agreed to meet with her.

One December night my mom and I drove an hour north to see this lady. We pulled into a gravel driveway and up to an old mansion in a nice part of town. There was a sign hanging on the door that said, "Ring doorbell and come in." I wiped my gray boots on the door mat, pressed the rusted doorbell and walked inside. I expected the house to smell musty since from the outside it looked like it had been built back in the early 1900s, but instead it smelled warm and welcoming.

This wasn't your typical house. Usually there's a dining room table to your left and a living room straight ahead. Instead, ten feet slightly to my right was a 15-foot-long wooden table. I felt like I was walking into a house where important people sat and made important decisions.

"Dr. H," as everyone affectionately called her, appeared out of nowhere. I don't know what I expected her to look like, but this wasn't it. She was white-haired with small spectacles resting on her nose. She had to be barely five feet tall and no more than 90 pounds.

"Please, come sit!" she said, pointing to the end of the table closest to us. For the next hour and a half, Dr. H explained how she had helped many successful people figure out what to do with their lives. Over the next several months, through hundreds of aptitude tests, we would identify my strengths and weaknesses and match those with jobs. I was clueless and wanted help. This sounded great to me. My mom and I told Dr. H goodbye and walked out to our car.

"Well, what do you think?" my mom asked me as we pulled out of the rocky dirt driveway.

"Let's do it."

A month later, I walked through the same door again and sat down at the table. Dr. H handed me a five-inch binder that could have been a weight at the gym. I knew instantly she meant business. Over the next three months, I took hundreds of aptitude tests, while we matched up my skills with certain careers.

Dr. H had what she affectionally called "skills groups." They consisted of six to eight people who were like me, clueless about what they wanted to do in the future. Together, the group would take tests, compare results, and do group exercises.

I showed up to my first skills group one night. I remember

walking in and receiving a sideways glance from everyone at the table. They were at least 20 years older than I and I could see they were hesitant that a 17-year-old with zero life experience was joining the group. I didn't belong.

It took a few meetings, but pretty soon I figured out that we were all sitting in an old house with a 90-year-old career counselor at a 15-foot table for the same reason: we were all trying to figure out what the heck we wanted to do with our lives.

One guy worked in an office, but had a passion for flipping houses on the side. Another guy worked as a financial consultant but after being a grandfather, discovered he loved working with kids. Others were completely clueless about what they wanted to do. Suddenly the 15-foot-long wooden table wasn't a place of fear and comparison. The table became a place of encouragement. It didn't matter what hard conversations or challenges we had faced that day. At 6 pm on Wednesday nights, we gathered around and told each other who we were.

Dr. H had us do a lot of different tests at that wooden table, but there was one that was my favorite. She would ask us to think of a time when we were proud of ourselves and share it with the group. The rest of the group held a stack of Dr. H's old business cards. While one person talked, the rest of us would write down characteristics that we saw the person had in the story (bravery, honesty, leadership, etc.). After the person was done sharing, we would go around the table and read through the words on the business cards, and each person would explain why they picked each word.

Retelling stories that made me proud of myself reminded me who I was. During my first meeting, I was losing at the game of comparison. Everyone was older, more experienced, more accomplished, and more intimidating. But after sitting around a table every week for two hours and discovering who these men and women wanted to be through their stories, I would drive home at night and feel honored I even had a seat at the table.

It was one thing to read the results of an aptitude test, but it was another thing to listen to the person sitting across from you speak words of affirmation and tell you who you were. Today, I still have every single business card stacked in my room, held together by two over-stretched rubber bands.

I long for a table like the one at Dr. H's house. A table where people can come and feel welcomed and loved and wanted and seen. I had a dream once that I had a 15-foot table in Nashville and some really cool people sitting at it. I could hear the hum of steady conversation and could see heads thrown back in laughter. I could sense the power of genuine community. Maybe I'll be sitting at that table one day. I hope so.

Right now, I don't have a fancy house to host people, or even some glass plates. But I have a wooden table that will fit six if we squeeze, white paper plates, and plastic silverware in the cabinet so no one has to do the dishes. And I'm starting with that.

CHAPTER 10

LESS WORDS,
MORE LOVE

I had no interest in going. It was Christmas Day and I was wrapped in a blanket snuggled next to my sister on the couch. The tree was lit and ripped wrapping paper that missed the trash can was scattered on the floor. My hair was still a mess and my legs were in plaid pajamas. My mouth watered as I fit the middle of a warm cinnamon roll into my mouth. Leaving the house in this rainy weather was the last thing on my mind. My dad had asked us a couple days before if we were interested in going to the homeless shelter and distributing clothes, shoes, and any other donations. Each of us had nodded a yes, but now I wasn't interested. It was Christmas, after all. The day when it's socially acceptable to stay on the couch all day.

As we were getting ready to leave the house, I watched my dad shove the $100 bill my grandma had sent him for Christmas into his left pocket. "Hey," he said, addressing all four of us. "I'm bringing my $100 with us. God might ask us to give it away. I would bring yours too in case He asks."

I turned around to face him and answered matter-of-factly. "I don't normally like giving homeless people money."

"If God prompts you to give it away, you should never say no," he answered.

"Lauren," I heard God say. *"Quit limiting Me to your minute expectations. I can do big things when people just say yes."*

"Quit putting Me in your box," He was saying. I'm good at that. When I feel uncomfortable, I cover up my fear by believing God is powerless. I shove Him in the glass box I feel trapped in sometimes.

I remembered another conversation He and I had when in fear, I doubted His power. *"I do the impossible as a lifestyle, Lauren."*

I knew He was right, but left my $100 sitting on the living room table anyway. Our white Suburban pulled out of the driveway.

The parking lot was packed. I found it ironic that we were meeting in the parking lot of the most popular haunted house in town. I leaned over and whispered to my mom, "A place of so much darkness gets to see light today."

She nodded.

Wrapped around the gated fence surrounding the edges of the parking lot was a line of homeless people waiting to get inside. I wasn't sure what to expect. I'd encountered and talked to and even prayed over homeless people before, but I had never seen this many at one time together outside the streets of Ft. Worth. The lead pastor apologized for not having anything specific for us to do.

"I'm sorry. There's nothing we absolutely need you to do," he said. "But go love people. Meet them and hear their stories. And thanks for being here today." Sometimes we get so caught up in the mission that we forget why we even came in the first place.

To my left on the concrete lay rows and rows of donated shoes. There were kids' shoes no longer than the length of my index finger and women's slippers I could fit two feet in. Dress shoes, slippers, sneakers, all lined up ready to be taken and worn some more.

An hour flew by. I was franticly hunting for a pair of men's dress shoes when I looked over to my right. A brown-headed, short volunteer walked up to the start of the shoe pile. No older than I, he took off his clean, new shoes and placed them next to the men's pile without a single word.

Just white socks covering his feet, he walked away on the chunky concrete with a small smile of joy on his face ready to seek out someone else who needed help. And he was ready to give it, even if it meant the shoes on his feet.

Tears filled my eyes. *What if we gave freely like that?* I wondered. I was ready to give away my shoes.

Not a minute later, the shoes he gave were in the hands of a tall, thin man who needed warm shoes. If only he knew.

Another man approached my brother and asked if we had any size 10.5 left. Most of the bigger sizes had been taken, so my brother shook his head. Then I watched as he kneeled down and began untying his own Adidas. "Here," he said, holding the shoes out to the man. "These should fit."

Immediately another woman approached the shortened rows of shoes. "I'm looking for a size 7.5 in tennis shoes," she whispered. I stepped across the row and slipped off mine. "These are exactly what you're looking for," I said. She shook her head and held up another pair. "Those are yours," she exclaimed. "These will work," pointing to the well-worn pair of tennis shoes she held in her hand. "No ma'am, I want you to have these," I said and slipped them in her trash bag.

My eyes filled with tears again. Two hours before I hadn't even been willing to leave my couch, and now I was walking around in socks trying to miss the sharp gravel dispersed along the concrete. I turned around to see a woman my age facing me across the rows of women's shoes. "Hi, I'm a reporter for a local newspaper. I saw what you did just now," she said. "Why did you do it?"

I could only smile and think of the man who led by example. Without a word, he had slipped off what looked like new shoes, maybe shoes he had even gotten that very morning as a gift. But what struck me was how he chose to give. Wordlessly. There wasn't an opportunity for praise. He wasn't looking for attention but saw an opportunity to be love.

If only she knew the example of selfless love I had witnessed moments earlier. She should have been interviewing him. They're just shoes. Replaceable. Shoes will rip and tear and get muddy and fall apart one day, but the look of shock on that man's face when Conner reached down and began untying his own shoes? I'll never forget it.

He is more valuable than the shoes on our feet.

After the reporter finished interviewing us, I walked across the parking lot to find the man who had led by example. I turned to my right and saw him a few feet away. "I saw what you did," I said. "And you're not the only one," I said with a smile as I glanced down at my socks. "Hi, I'm Lauren."

"I'm Mitch."

"Thank you for being love." His face exploded with a smile

and he gave me a huge hug.

"Never lose that joy," he exclaimed as I looked back and smiled.

When my family walked back to our car that afternoon, only one of us was wearing shoes.

A couple weeks later, a friend pointed out something I hadn't noticed. "Lauren," she said. "I love how God knows exactly the right ways to speak to our individual hearts. Your dad's willingness to give away his money was his thing, but giving away the shoes off your feet was yours." Even in my rebellious decision to leave my cash at home, God had another plan to capture my heart. And little did I know it wouldn't require money, but a small homeless woman in the middle of a parking lot in Ft. Worth and a pair of pink Adidas shoes.

My new friend Mitch didn't have to tell people what he was going to do. He just did it.

Like Mitch, I'm trying to be less talk and more love. More like Jesus.

• • •

My dad led a business club at my school. Every year before Christmas break, he offered a challenge to each member. Each person received $5 and, if we accepted, we had to figure out a way to turn the $5 into $20. If not, my dad asked that we put the money in the offering plate at church or use the money to bless someone. As dedicated as I was to the club, I didn't take the challenge. Until senior year. As my dad handed out the money, I scolded myself for waiting so long. I was going to do it this year. I needed to get over my fear of failure and embarrassment and just do it. A week before Christmas on a Sunday night, I decided it was time.

I went to Target and bought a box of cake mix for $1.08. My mom insisted I make homemade icing (apparently store-bought is a disgrace) and use cupcake liners that we had at home, so I did. My sister made the homemade icing, and I threw the cupcake mix in a bowl and shoved the pan in the oven. Twenty minutes later they were ready, and my impatient self was ready to throw on some icing and head out the door, but Hannah and my mom insisted that they look good. I rolled my eyes. After all, we weren't looking to win Cupcake Wars. I just needed to make $20.

After the cupcakes were decorated, I put 20 of them on a cute plastic platter and headed out the door. If I needed more, I could always go back to my house. My plan was to tell my neighbors about the club challenge and sell each cupcake for $1. I turned to my left and decided I wanted to start at the houses where I knew the neighbors a little better. I didn't want to get rejected at the first door I went to.

I stood on my neighbor's front porch and rang the doorbell. The door swung open a couple minutes later, and I began my 30-second elevator speech I rehearsed in my head. "Hi, Mr. Griffin! I'm Lauren Kinney and I'm participating in a challenge from my business club at school. I have to turn $5 into $20, so I made these cupcakes and I'm selling them for $1 a piece. Would you like to buy one?" Mr. Griffin smiled and pulled out a couple $1 bills from his pocket. "I'll take three." he said. As I handed him a plate of cupcakes, Mrs. Griffin came to the door and handed me $5. Boom. I had made $8. Surely this wouldn't be too hard.

I walked across the street to the Lewis's house. Mr. Lewis answered the door and I repeated my elevator speech all over again with a smile. He looked down at the platter of cupcakes in my hands and said the four craziest words I've ever hear.

"I'll buy them all."

My eyes got five sizes bigger and my mouth hung open. "How many do you have?" he asked. "I have 20 with me sir, and 28 at my house." He took a few steps back inside and came back to the door. In his hand was a $100 bill.

"Take them to all of the neighbors on the street," he said. I was dumbfounded. "Yes sir. Thank you, sir. Thank you so much,

Mr. Lewis." He took a cupcake off my tray and shut the door.

I was shocked. Surely I was dreaming. This was unreal. I did the most awkward run-walk back to my house, trying to balance my tray of cupcakes and grasping my $100 bill that had been so freely given to me. I threw open the front door to my house and ran inside to proclaim the news to my family. They were shocked. But my dad just smiled. An hour later, every house on our street had received three red velvet cupcakes with homemade icing, "courtesy of Mr. Lewis."

I was in disbelief the rest of the week. The Griffins had been very generous to give me $8 for three cupcakes made with cheap cake mix and homemade icing.

But wow. It wasn't the $100 that blew me away. Okay, maybe a little. It was the fact that Mr. Lewis had me deliver them to all the neighbors on the street, which allowed me to see the result of generosity: the joy on our neighbors' faces. I was honored to be a part of it.

I walked out into that cold December night with a platter of cheap cupcakes and walked away with $108. Later that week, I wrote my dad an email, as we were formally required to do, still shaking my head at what had happened.

What struck me wasn't the money—it was how Mr. Lewis didn't ask me how many cupcakes I had first, as if he would have considered the amount before deciding if they were worth $100. No. He bought all of them anyway, not knowing how many I had. Mr. Lewis' selfless action reminds me of Jesus' love for us.

Mr. Lewis freely gave me a gift. He didn't ask to be recognized but was anyway. And let me see the return on his generosity. What if I lived my life this way?

Mr. Lewis freely gave. I want to freely give like that.

With some help, we can take a little and turn it into a lot. Can you see the headline now? "Below-average baker with cheap cupcakes meets neighbor with a generous spirit and loving heart." "One little boy with three loaves and a fish meets a miracle provider." But they were both world-changers, regardless of what they had, all because someone was willing to invest in them. Just like how Mr. Lewis was generous, Jesus performed extraordinary miracles out of ordinary things.

I don't think Jesus is looking for the most extravagant acts of selflessness. He's looking for less words and more love. It was never about the words or affirmation anyway.

• • •

Maggie and I went to grab fro-yo one day. Having just gotten the first year of college under our belt, we had a lot to catch up on. We talked regularly, but the distance between

Alabama and Texas didn't allow the luxury of regular coffee or fro-yo conversations. As I swirled my sweet caramel yogurt around with my spoon, she began talking about the unlikely friendships she's made in college. "I've become best friends with three women who work in the dining hall near my dorm," she said.

"Lauren, so many people are rude to them. They won't look them in the eye when ordering food. They're treated like complete inconveniences. It's terrible." Maggie looked up from her cup of frozen yogurt and shook her head. "No one should be treated that way, especially by the people that they're serving." Every time Maggie goes into the cafeteria, she intentionally looks them in the eye and asks how their day is. She remembers their names. She even asks how she can pray for them.

And they know her. Maggie's bright, blonde hair makes her stand out. And her huge smile is hard to forget. But the three ladies in the cafeteria don't know Maggie by her brilliance, research on childhood development studies, or that she leads with one of the most impactful organizations on campus. They know Maggie for her love. And in that love, they see Jesus.

"Lauren, we don't have to do a handstand to show people love."

Maggie's right. We don't have to dazzle people with our love. Jesus didn't go around with a traveling circus doing tricks or mastering the trapeze while people marveled at His abilities. Somewhere along the way we picked up this notion that love has to be flashy, pretty, pleasing, and posted on Instagram. Love was never intended to impress, but to be freely given.

· · ·

Every year, my family and I take a summer vacation. We always have a really, really hard time picking a place to go. Five out of the six people in our herd love the beach. So who's the loser? It's me. It's not that I don't like the beach, but I just love the city more. While lying in the burning hot sun and reapplying sunscreen every two minutes sounds like a blast, I prefer a city skyline with a Starbucks cup in hand.

When I picture the beach, I see myself lying on a beach towel in a cute swimsuit getting the perfect tan, running barefoot across the shoreline, and swimming in clear waters where I can see my feet as if I were starring in a movie. Instead, I end up forgetting my flip flops, forcing myself to do high knees across the beach in a poor effort not to sear my feet from the burning coals below them. I also usually forget my sunglasses and a hat, leaving my nose cooking in the sun.

We have a certain system for deciding the location for our family vacations. Each of us gets to suggest a place and then we narrow down the options. It always comes down to the beach and my suggestion—so five against one and the beach always wins. But this past summer, somehow I won out, and dragged my family to New York City. Maybe my parents felt bad for me. Regardless, I was excited to return to the magical city of taxi cabs and advertisements the size of my house, where pizza and pushy people can be found on every street corner.

We happened to be there on the Fourth of July, so my mom bought tickets for our family to take a ferry to the Statue of Liberty. I don't think it gets more patriotic than that.

The pedestal of the statue was packed full of people of every kind. I was amazed at how many people were on Ellis Island celebrating the holiday—it was like one huge birthday party. I kind of hope mine is that big someday. Our family found a spot on the ledge, snapped some pics, and admired the view. You could see all from New York City to New Jersey from up there. It was beautiful.

My dad whispered to the four of us, "See how many people you can get to wave back at you," and the competition was on. Our hands shook wildly for 20 straight minutes.

"Get the lady in the red by the railing!"

"The dude in the stripes—he looks friendly!"

"What about the girl in the blue shirt? Has anyone gotten her?"

We started pointing at people and waving like they were old friends we hadn't seen in years. We didn't care—we were making people smile (and probably freaking a few of them out).

Our family had just walked down from the pedestal of the statue when a security guard yelled above us, "Evacuate the statue immediately!" My mom yelled at my brothers and Hannah, who had wandered off to take some more pictures, and we walked quickly towards the stairs leading down to the ground level of the island.

Directly in front of me, I watched a security guard tell a woman, "Someone's climbing the statue." My head whipped back to my right and looked up. Sure enough, someone was sitting in the crevice right by Lady Liberty's foot.

The six of us found ourselves in front of the small building behind the statue where the lockers and security checkpoints were. Packed in with hundreds of our new friends, we found a spot with a clear view of the back of the statue, but all we could see were the security guards gathered around the spot where the climber was.

I figured that this was a somewhat normal occurrence. I

mean, surely this person had not been the first to climb the Statue of Liberty. I was sure the park rangers and security guards knew how to handle this and that we would be back up taking selfies with the Lady herself in no time. I was wrong.

The area was filling up with people, all asking the same questions while taking as many pictures and videos as they could. Even the staff at the gift shop and cafe were pointing fingers towards the green sculpture. No one was leaving. After about 30 minutes, security ordered the entire island to be evacuated. Police rushed by and then men with fancy helmets with ropes in hand ran past us and up towards the statue. Paramedics followed minutes later with a stretcher. Two police helicopters swarmed loudly above our heads, flying in close circles above the statue. This was serious.

We gradually moved towards the dock as eight security guards walked in a semicircle in front us, forming a blockade. The crowd was still enthralled by their surroundings. Every person still had their phone in hand, snapping away as if their iPhone camera could see through the giant tree that had hidden the statue from view.

I turned around to the officer standing directly behind me. "Sir, has this ever happened before?"

"Nope. This is the first time anyone has ever intentionally attempted to climb the statue."

My jaw dropped as my eyebrows raised. "Really?"

"Yes. There was a man who was paragliding who was accidentally blown onto the statue. He was hanging from the torch. Not a pretty sight. But that was back before 9/11. No one's ever climbed it like this."

There was more than a headlining news story unravelling before our eyes—history was being made. After waiting an hour or so, we boarded the ferry and headed back to the shore. Although the island was now empty, the curiosity of the tourists hadn't decreased for a second. I was right there with them, updating my Instagram story with videos of the person sitting on the statue from all angles. Every head was turned facing the statue on the boat ride back, as the two police helicopters roared above our heads. We watched as two policemen made their way up to the person, peeked their heads over the ledge, and began engaging in dialogue with the woman.

If you would have told me that I would be evacuated from Ellis Island in the middle of the biggest news story in America on the Fourth of July, and interviewed on CBS2, I would have laughed in your face. Yet here I was, standing on the shoreline of New York City with a foam microphone in my face talking about what happened hours earlier.

On the ferry ride over to Ellis Island, all I wanted was a

nice, quiet Fourth of July, a selfie with Lady Liberty (hard to get in New York City in the first place), and a break from the humidity. The wind breezed through my hair and the only thing I was worried about was not dropping my sunglasses or phone into the ocean. Instead I ended up witnessing the biggest (and highest elevated) crime scene in New York City on the Fourth of July. And there was no wind in my hair on the way back. Just a lot of sweaty people. As we got off the boat, I glanced back to the statue and could barely make out three little specks just above the ledge: the two policemen and the woman.

Three hours later, the two policemen were finally able to get the woman down from the statue in a harness and safely lower her back to the ground. What sacrificial love. Despite hanging out on a steep ledge thousands of feet up in the air, the two men weren't distracted by the loud news helicopters above their heads live streaming their every move or the thousands of people gathered around the statue in line to be evacuated. They cared about one thing: the safety of the woman.

The woman's safety was the last thing I was thinking about. I think I would have told her, "Girl! You got yourself up there, you can get yourself down!" But those two policemen who spent three hours towering over New York City in harnesses were only trying to get the woman safely on the ground. It reminds me a lot of the love that Jesus has for us.

He doesn't care how high He has to go. No matter the things that you've walked through, the shame that you've carried, and the worthlessness that you've believed about yourself, He jumps in the pit with you. He loves you. To Him you are never worthless. He's been walking beside you all along. You have always been worth something to Him.

He is kind and patient and He waits. Not for us to have it all together, but He meets us where we are. The men had no tie to that woman. She wasn't their daughter, mother, wife, or even a friend. They knew once they lowered her to the ground, she wouldn't be thanking them for their risky rescue. But they climbed up anyway, demonstrating selfless patience and sacrifice for the sake of others.

Six months later, I was driving home one afternoon angry at a friend for hurtful comments he had made and questioned why I was even still friends with him. I began asking God why for the 1,000th time this year. Why we love the hard people and choose to keep loving them anyway. Why we fight for them anyway. I'll never forget His answer:

"Lauren," He whispered. "That was you."

"You ran. You hid. You wanted nothing to do with me. You shoved me in a drawer and left me on read."

"But I still fought for you. I fought anyway. And it was worth it."

"Fight for My people. It's hard. I would know."

I was reminded once again of the two men on the Statue of Liberty who waited anyway to rescue the woman.

I don't have the patience to wait the two minutes it takes to microwave Easy Mac, much less wait three hours for someone to get off the Statue of Liberty. But I'm so thankful for a God who does. Not only does He wait, but He meets us right where we are.

Even on the foot of the Statue of Liberty.

CHAPTER 11

NEVER ABOUT THE APPLAUSE

I watched his truck come to a quick halt at the stop sign and turn right. He was gone.

"I'm so sorry, Lauren," he had whispered. I stood there, frozen, and whispered a prayer over him anyway, like I had done for every friend who had ever driven away from my house.

I put one shoe in front of the other and walked slowly back up the sidewalk to my front door, in complete disbelief. *What had I done?* It didn't matter. It was over. Nothing could be fixed. My right hand reached out to open the door and I heard it.

"Lauren, when did I stop being enough for you?"

He was an unexpected gift from the beginning. I had come to Nashville looking to find myself and my big dreams, not a boyfriend. He was never in the plan. But weeks later, we were dating. I couldn't get over what a free gift he was. In fact, I asked God that a lot. "Why?" I would ask. "Why *now*? You knew I wasn't looking for a guy."

I couldn't get over the fact that I was now in a relationship, and suddenly, just a little over two months later, I was left standing empty-handed on a sidewalk as a part of me drove away. It had been freely given, and now it was taken away. I snapped back into the present and realized I was still standing at my front door. And now God was asking me a question. *"Lauren, when did I stop being enough for you?"*

Little did I know He would ask me that every day for the next three months. *"Lauren, when did this world become enough for you? When did he become enough for you? When did this become enough for you?"*

But in my disbelief about the gift I had been given, the gift had become more important than the gift-giver. I just didn't realize the gift was driving away on that May afternoon and all I had left was the gift-giver.

"Okay, God," I answered. "I am so excited to see Your plan in this."

I shut the door on rejection. I was actually just opening a new one. One of refinement.

• • •

I ran into Jason at Common Grounds during finals week. I was walking out of the bathroom when I saw his head pop out behind a chemistry book. "Lauren!"

"Jason! What's up?" We caught each other up on our semesters and he asked how my classes were going. "Honestly Jason, I hate school. This semester's been hard. Accounting's been hard. But this book. This book is what makes me want to get out of bed in the morning."

Jason smiled and gave me an update on his semester and how our other friends from high school were doing. "You know, Lauren, it's been such a joy to watch each of us find a little more of who we are and watch each other grow this semester. Carrie in nursing school, Austin on the football team, Lance is at Baylor, and you're writing a book. God is moving in each of us, and I'm just honored to watch it all unfold." I smiled, hugged him, and went back to my table. It wasn't until that night that I found myself repeating the words I had said to Jason.

The book is what makes me want to get out of bed in the morning. It wasn't the words themselves, but the way they had escaped my mouth. There was a deep pride and yearning for approval rooted in those words. As fast as I realized how arrogant my statement had been, I heard His voice.

"Really, Lauren? What about me?"

All my life, I've had to have a purpose. A project, a title, a goal. I was always working towards something: winning the class president election or being selected as the captain of the junior varsity volleyball team or raising money for a classmate or being a team leader at work. And people knew it. Talking with Jason that afternoon, I felt like I had to qualify my tanking accounting grade with writing a book. Prove my purpose and my worthiness. I was constantly trying to prove I was worth something. Someone worth celebrating.

I stood there in front of Jason that day thinking, *I know I'm not smart. I'm failing accounting right now and probably will have to re-take it. I'm embarrassed. Humiliated. Ashamed. I know my transcript looks bad, but guess what? I'm writing a book! Ever heard of a college student writing a book? Nope! I'm special! Look at me! I'm not worthless!* I stood there, nodding along to the words Jason was speaking and not hearing any of them because the voice in my head was screaming so loud. So loud I wondered if Jason could hear it. That was when the statement came tumbling out of my mouth: "This book is what makes me want to get out of bed in the morning."

The purpose of writing was never about qualifying myself.

In fact, writing has always been a place where the chains of approval break and Lauren Kinney is set free to be the imperfect yet real girl she's always been.

That night after talking to Jason, I realized writing this book was becoming a front for the failure I felt I was—and my failing accounting grade was just the surface. I was making excuses for working 30 hours a week, not joining a church, and spending the weekends alone at the Austin library when it felt like everyone else was spending time with their 50 friends and enjoying real community. I still didn't feel like I knew what that meant.

Defending and qualifying myself had become a natural habit, even mentally. I combatted worthlessness with pride. And it may look like a shiny sword, but it's guaranteed to break at the first swing.

The enemy wasn't just working to claim that lie over Jason's and my conversation that afternoon. He was working to persuade my mind and my heart that I could win the battle for love with the sword of approval. That I would be crowned with adoration and real love if I could just write more words and more pages and each of those things would equate to feeling worthy of affection and applause. Loved. Wanted. Accepted.

The enemy is good at giving the illusion of freedom. He

wants us to think we're loosening our chains by giving into the love of man, when God says we will truly be free when we give up our love affair with approval and applause and give into His love. Freedom comes with loss of control. Writing isn't what sets me free. It was never what broke the chains of approval and love and worth and value. He set me free a long time ago, but He's allowed me time and time again to express that love in writing.

At the root of it all, this book was always a dream. It was a dream given by God to glorify Him. But the enemy loves to twist and corrupt our dreams until it seems like if we don't achieve them, we lose the worthiness and love and adoration that the enemy wants us to think we've been lacking, when we've actually had it the entire time. We've had it all along.

I love how from the beginning of our conversation Jason wasn't gushing over our friends' achievements, but how Jesus allowed us to use them as a way to glorify Him. This book isn't who I am and this book doesn't rewrite my story. Jesus does. He sees me as worthy of such a sacrifice, as if the book never even mattered.

I think that might be everyone's goal in life. We want to be loved more for who we are rather than what we're doing. It's funny too, because we're doing these tangible things to prove that we're worth something—when all along we just wanted to be loved for who we are.

I often hear from God when I'm driving, so I've learned to keep a stack of sticky notes and a small notebook in one of the cup holders in my car (along with assorted pens). Earlier this summer, after God clearly asked me, *"When did I stop being enough for you?"* I was driving out of my neighborhood when I grabbed a sticky note and a pen and wrote this down: "When I know You are enough, You are everything I need."

For so long I believed the manuscript was a completely different type of paper. It was my words. No accounting equations or grades at the top in red pen or bland bubble sheets and No. 2 pencils. It was mine to write. But the book isn't eternal. Neither are my big dreams to move to Nashville and love people. Or my future husband or kids. This isn't eternal. Jesus is. And Jesus is what makes this book worth writing. People worth pursuing. Love worth staying. Life worth living.

I've been wrong my entire life. Growing up in the church, I knew God was kind and merciful and patient. But some part of me refused to believe His love was a gift freely given. It was completely against the mantra my mind knew: you will earn the love you receive. All along, I never had to prove I was worthy of being loved by a God so merciful and loving.

"Here's the deal," God is saying. *"You never had to have a*

plan, a purpose, or a roadmap for Me to love you and think you're worth something. Lauren, you've been worth something to Me all along."

I want you to know that today too. You've been worth something all along.

My sister once told me, "God doesn't compare. He just creates."

I was flying back to Dallas from LA. I had just finished meeting with a friend about the book and for the first time in a while, I felt unstuck. New ideas and content were floating around my head, and my fingers couldn't move fast enough to get them all down. But when I pulled out my laptop on the plane, my fingers froze and I stared blankly at my computer. All of the emotions of joy and confusion and excitement set in, and I couldn't move. So I just sat there and cried. A few days before, I had seen a friend post on Instagram about writing her third book and how many times she had wanted to give up. I remember holding my phone and laughing, not at her, but at myself, because my moment hadn't come yet. But right there on the plane, the moment came and I started to think, *Is it even worth it? All of this. Is it even worth it?*

It was two o'clock in the morning when I started my blog. I was sitting at my kitchen table with my mom next to me, throwing around names. It just couldn't be something cheesy.

Honestly, what I ended up picking was kind of cheesy, but it was three in the morning at that point and I wanted to go to bed. "A Girl and Her Words," my mom suggested, to which I lovingly replied, "If I wake up and hate it, I'll change it in the morning." I never did. Four years later I'm still writing on that blog and some of those crazy stories are what got me writing this book.

Writing that blog wasn't always rewarding.

It was August and I was back home in Waco for my sophomore year. The day after I posted a blog, I invited a few close friends over for ice cream. As we sat around my kitchen counter talking about our summers, my phone vibrated. It was Ben, one of my high school friends. I glanced down and read the text silently. "This one is better than the last one you sent me."

I sat there and continued listening to my friends talk about their summers and tried to hold back the tears that had started to form in my eyes. It hurt. *I should have seen it coming*, I told myself, and thought back to the first time I had gotten the courage to text him the link and how he had responded.

"The font's nice," he had said. Ben's text was between several others that said, "Lauren, thank you for writing this," or "Beautiful writing, LK!" But it is funny to me that when

I think back to writing that blog, Ben's voice is the only one I seem to hear. How is it possible to be distracted by one lie that rests among 50 truths?

One night in junior high, I came home and locked myself in my room with the lights off. I don't remember what had happened that made me so angry, but in the pitch-black darkness, I managed to grab a pen and my journal and write a list of words I believed about myself. Words like unlovable, trash, and unwanted stared back at me.

I remember sitting there in the corner shoved between the wall and my door and with every mark of my pen the enemy's presence became stronger in my room. Nothing made him feel more powerful than in that moment. I think back to that night and wish I would have realized the grave of lies I was digging. I've learned that the enemy wants us to affirm who we are in what we often falsely believe we are.

Now, when I feel like I've failed and deserve a consequence, I remember. I remember my consequence is what Jesus died for. He paid it all. No punishment. No more.

I remember the first time I heard that an ex-boyfriend was dating someone else. I was so angry, but instead of locking myself in the darkness with the lie that I wasn't good enough, I put on a pair of running shoes and ran five miles. I allowed that anger to fuel a conversation with truth and the God who defines it.

As my feet pounded the pavement, God kept saying, *"Lauren! Quit believing the lie that you aren't good enough because you, even as angry and sweaty as you are right now, are enough for Me. I am all that matters. When will you start believing it?"*

Even today, I can be distracted by one lie when Jesus is telling me 300 truths.

A friend reminded me recently, "Jesus' truth has been around for 2,000+ years. That dude has been alive for 20ish. Whose word are you going to trust more?"

Who are you going to believe?

I still text Ben the link when I write. Every time I pray that he will do more than just glance at the font. It takes some courage on my part to press send, but I think it takes Ben more courage to open it, and I thank God for that. Words still hurt. They always will. But I send Ben the link anyway because I'm not looking for affirmation from anyone but Jesus. I want the ink I bleed to glorify my Father. I want my story to be His, and it doesn't matter what anyone else thinks.

For a long time, I believed the lie that I had to be doing something to be worth something. And it's not true. This is the hard fact I am learning right now. It is a choice, a fight, every day, and it's never as glorious as I pictured it. The enemy battles hard for my heart just like he does for yours, and he won't stop until we become convinced that God simply isn't enough for us.

First and foremost, I was made to love Him. And if I'm not doing that well, then what are all my efforts for? I want to live a life that pleases Him. It can't be about the applause. It can't be for anyone but Him. I was made to live for an audience of One.

Hannah and I were sitting at our favorite local coffee shop one afternoon when I asked her to read the first draft of the book. I sat there sipping my chocolate milk, waiting for her to look back at me with the "Oh my gosh, Lauren, this is incredible, I just want to cry" sister look. Instead, Hannah looked back at me and gave me the most condescending glance I've ever seen. It read, "Lauren, this sucks." And she was right. It did. So I trashed the whole thing and started over. Much to my shock, God was using her to tell me, *"These words are to glorify Me and not you."*

It's taken me a long time to learn it was never about the applause. The affirmation. I wanted so badly. I wanted to be valued. Loved. Worth something. Seen as a world-changer. But after talking to Jason that night, it hit me. It is all for Him. And He just has to be enough. So I'm doing it. I'm writing this dang book. But it's no longer for anyone else but Him.

• • •

I have a sticky note that's placed right above my document when I write. It has one sentence: Was Lauren Kinney always going places or was Lauren Kinney always running towards Jesus?

One afternoon while I was a junior in high school, I decided to go on a run. It was a crisp, fall afternoon and absolutely beautiful outside so I laced up my tennis shoes, grabbed my earphones, and started running. Let me set the record straight: I didn't end up with the marathon genes from my incredible mother. I don't shoot for much. Around three miles or however long my body can go without dying is usually the goal.

After the first mile that day, I could feel my legs becoming sore so I whispered harshly to my heart, "Get it together, Lauren. You are stronger than this." As I made a loop around the block, I saw my sister outside and refused to tell her I could only do one mile. Stubborn Lauren at her finest. I knew I had to keep my feet moving.

They didn't stop. Ninety minutes later, I was nine miles in and knew for a fact that I wasn't doing this on my own. I kept circling back to my house, thinking surely my feet would give out and I would go inside. But each time I passed my driveway, the desire to keep running became stronger and stronger. I was exhausted. Definitely dehydrated. The sun had gone down long ago. But I was nowhere near ready to stop running. My phone had just buzzed at the 9.5-mile mark when I pulled my phone out of my arm strap and saw that I had missed 10 phone calls from my mom. I called her back, out of breath, and she demanded that I come home immediately. I pleaded with her to let me reach 10 miles, but she wouldn't hear it. I turned around and started running home, head hung low in disappointment.

There was no way my mom's concern for my safety was going to crush my now so-close dream of running 10 miles without stopping. So I started running up and down the entryway to my house. The short sidewalk was only about 50 feet long. After what seemed like 200 mini-sprints I finished. 10.3 miles.

Whenever I look at the sticky note on my laptop, I think of the 10.3 miles I ran that day. I figured out three miles in that God wasn't carrying my feet so that Hannah would applaud me when I got home.

"Lauren," He was saying. "You run to glorify Me only and I will always carry your feet."

That's one of my favorite things about following Jesus. We

just need a good pair of shoes and a voice we trust.

My mom ran a marathon a couple years ago and said it's one of the hardest things she's ever done (besides raise four kids). For months, I watched her prepare to run 26.2 miles in one day. She changed her diet, bought really ugly running shoes that were only meant to be worn by hardcore people, and ran every day. For months. Each day getting closer and closer to her goal of running across that finish line.

On the day of the race, the rest of my family climbed into the car and drove to the starting line to cheer my mom on. There weren't a ton of people at the start line. Maybe because it was 7 a.m., but I figured I would do anything, including waking up early, to see someone I loved do something they've worked hard to do. For the next five hours, we tracked my mom around the course, driving and parking on random streets. We waved signs and cheered her on as well as the others who ran before, beside, and behind her.

Six hours later, my dad parked the car, and the five of us jumped out and ran to the finish line where runners had just started coming in, waiting for a lady in bright colored leggings and a beanie to cross under an overhang of balloons and a huge sign that said "FINISH." We stood there, necks craning and eyes searching for one person. No one else mattered. Just our mom.

I'll never forget when I saw her. Her face was bright red and she was out of breath, but ever so gracefully in step. Hannah and the boys and I screamed, "MOM!" at the top of our lungs and she turned her head to the right and saw us. Feet trembling but her fist pumping as if it were the only thing propelling her forward, my mom crossed the finish line and fell to the ground a few feet later, trying to catch her breath and regain her balance.

She ran to my dad first, tears streaming down her face. They didn't have to say anything. They knew it all. My mom took off her shoes in the car and what I saw made me light-headed. Each of her toes was doubled in size, black and purple, with high blisters. It was gross, but my mom didn't care. She had finished the race. Nothing else mattered.

When I think about the moment when we'll see Jesus someday, I picture my mom running across the finish line at the Cowtown and my dad sweeping her off her feet. Jesus is there, and not just at the start line or the finish line or at one pit stop when we have to go to the bathroom. He's there all the time, running beside us. He's not patting us on the back or throwing us a towel to wipe the beads of sweat on our foreheads. He's in front of us, looking us in the eyes and saying, *"You can do this. I'm right here. You got this."*

When we trip on the rock we didn't see, He'll catch us.

When we take the wrong turn, He'll point us back to the right direction. Even when we know the map and we see a shortcut that will save us time and energy, He shakes His head and smiles while offering His hand and says, *"My way is better."*

I still think it's crazy how many more people there were at the finish line than at the starting line. A lot of people want to be there for the glory moments and the celebration, but not many are willing to be present from the very beginning, even before the runner hits the pavement. Those are the people who truly understand every mile and sweaty laundry load it took to cross the finish line. Jesus is one of those people too. He's been cheering you on for a long time, and I don't think He plans on stopping until you're in His arms.

Following Jesus doesn't come with a stack of cash or a promise to be rich and famous. A fancy car isn't waiting for you at the finish line and neither is a cool T-shirt or a group of photographers and journalists asking your secret to success. Instead it comes with a fire and a family. Guts and faith. Failure but a finish line. And maybe a few bloodied, bruised toes along the way.

• • •

At the root of it all, it was never about the applause. It

was about earning love. It's funny the lengths we'll go. We'll drive and fly a lot of miles, write a lot of words, and fake relationships with other people all searching for one real thing: love. I think this might be everyone's goal in life. We're just pursuing it in 7.6 billion different ways. And He's pursuing our hearts in 7.6 billion different ways.[5]

We're trying to prove what we're worth in what we're doing, when all along we just want to be loved for who we are. And He knows that. That's why Jesus didn't come to the world to give away money and put on a show. He saw who people were, even the parts they couldn't yet see themselves, and loved them anyway. I still don't have it all figured out, but I think I got this part down: the love I've tried so hard to earn has been a free gift all along. And He loves me regardless of whether I write this book.

People talk about surrender like it's a one-time fight. It isn't. I wake up every single morning and pray that I run towards Jesus. Every single day I want to bask in the affirmation and love of anyone but Him. I fail. I fail a lot. In fact, I'm amazed that Jesus hasn't given up on me. He never berates me but treats me like a father would. When a child starts walking for the first time, wide-eyed parents watch in amazement. When their child falls, they don't get angry. They applaud, cheer, smile and yell, "You got this! Get back up again!" and set you back on your feet. He's the same way with you and me. We're bound to fail and He knows that. And He, if we let Him, puts us back on our feet too.

For my 19th birthday, my dad gave me a set of children's novels entitled *Choose Your Own Adventure*. Each book is written in second-person with the reader as the main character. Every couple of pages, the reader gets to pick from a few options how he wishes to continue the story. They were my dad's favorite books when he was a kid, and he was obsessed with the idea that he had the power to choose his own story. I think the books, in a lot of ways, are like our lives. Ultimately, we get to choose which direction we drive our cars, which way we walk to class, what food we eat, and the clothes we wear. We get to pick who we marry, who we spend our time with, and how we want to spend it. We get to pick our own adventure.

At the end of the day, we're all writing a story. The words we speak, miles we drive, steps we take, letters we type, pictures we post, and minutes we waste. Yours could be a million pages long, but it's the one paragraph at the end that truly matters: who you are and where you're going and how you're leading people along the way.

Were you always going places or were you always running towards Jesus?

. . .

In December of 2018, God told me explicitly to take a break from Instagram. It wasn't, "Hey, Lauren, maybe you should consider spending less time on Instagram." It was, *"Lauren, I want you to get off for three months."* There wasn't a hint of give in His voice. I knew what He had said. And I said no.

I remember standing there in the shower, thinking of how I had to be using social media to promote myself, my blog and my book. Taking three months off was never on the table. This was never part of the plan.

So I told Him, "No." I did. I stepped out of the shower and while ignoring His statement, I asked Him another question: "Why is following You so hard?" I think it's a question we're all dying to ask. I don't care who you are—God asks everyone to do things that make us want to throw our hands in the air and ask, "What's the point?" People love to talk about how many times they've said yes to God, but no one's talking about the no's it took to get to the yes.

"Why is following You so hard?"

He took no time to respond.

"If following Me was easy, you would have said yes the first

time, Lauren. "And a month and a half later, His words still lingered in my mind. I gave in to my will when I should have surrendered to His—the first time.

It's funny how for so long, I wanted to be visible. I wanted people to know what I was doing, where I was flying on the weekends, and who I was sitting across the table from. I wanted them to feel like they were dancing with me at the 15 concerts I went to one semester and enjoying the avocado toast I was eating for brunch in Los Angeles. Exposure meant value, and value meant love. And now God was asking me to go dark in the middle of what seemed to me the very time to come alive. The one thing I had spent the past year and a half learning to avoid was what He was now asking me to sit in for three months. It wasn't to look fear in the face and say, "I'm braver than you" one last time, but He was asking me to get so close to my fear of invisibility that I might as well get BFF necklaces for both of us. It was time for me to become friends with fear.

Weeks passed by and I hated every moment I was missing out on. I had a friend from Austin run her first marathon and several friends get engaged. I missed prom pictures and state championships and weddings and pregnancy announcements and friends having babies.

There was one weekend where I remember lying in bed

thinking about what would happen if I forgot my Instagram password and couldn't log back in. Even a month in, I still desperately wanted control and couldn't bear to think of losing connections with the followers I had. Even if I lost all of those "friends" and Jesus was all I had left, would He really be enough?

The next month, I was asked to speak at a worship night for a women's business organization. When I started asking God what He wanted me to speak about, He said, *"Lauren, I want you to tell My daughters that I see them."* I nearly laughed. A month before, that would have meant absolutely nothing to me. But now the irony of it all was hilarious. God was teaching me that even when the world told me I was invisible, He saw me, and stripping away Instagram was the first step. God sees you when the world doesn't. It was supposed to be this way all along.

I'll never forget two of my friends' responses when they asked why I deleted Instagram. "Why?" they asked.

"God told me to and I said no," I would say in response.

Shaking their heads, they looked at me and said, "Well Lauren, you should never tell God no. That never goes down very well." I never expected to feel shamed for telling God no the first time, but to be affirmed and encouraged in the fact that I was now choosing to listen and obey. How many times am I tearing down others because they also didn't say yes the first time?

I tell God no every day. When I don't call that person He put on my heart or when I don't speak kindly to the barista at Starbucks. When I choose to sleep a little longer instead of spending time reading in my Bible or praying. Right now, I'm working on affirming people to reconsider their no's. And yes, when we believe the Holy Spirit is speaking, we should act on it—the first time.

God takes our no's anyway and is so rich in mercy and compassion that He chooses to freely give second chances like confetti. He uses our no's for redemptive yeses.

I was driving home one night when I heard Him ask me a question that summed up the entire reason I was off Instagram. It was a piercing blow and yet was such a kind revelation.

"Lauren, when will you stop trying to impress people and just become Mine?"

"Lauren," He was saying, *"When will you stop trying to find your identity in applause and approval and anyone's love but Mine? I've already set you free and proclaimed you are My daughter. When will you start living like it?"*

A wise friend once told me, "Beneath all the fear is all the freedom."

I think it might be okay to be invisible every once and a while.

CHAPTER 12

ALWAYS SUPPOSED TO BE THIS WAY

I recently traveled to Georgia to visit a college for my sister. As two tour guides wearing colorful name tags talked about their college experience with huge smiles plastered on their faces, I glanced around at the room of high school juniors and seniors. Faces eager to begin something new.

Freedom.

They have no idea what's ahead. And I am so glad I didn't know.

I had no idea what was coming. We're never given all the answers, but God promised me one thing: *"I don't abandon My children, Lauren."* And leaning into that promise and letting go of all else is what got me here.

I think back to that night standing in the foyer of my dorm as the guy sitting behind the front desk told me he wasn't my mom. He was right. It was time for me to know freedom.

The night Jason and Austin and I sang so loud in the car and praised Jesus for His faithfulness regardless of what we were feeling.

The night I left my room and slept peacefully for the first time in weeks on a couch that wasn't mine.

The night Jake and I broke up.

The January afternoon I sat in a cloth chair and signed a form dropping out of rush and showed up at my doorstep in Arlington.

The night I met Erin, my future roommate in a crowd of people.

The day Phil and Gina and I sat in a room full of sunlight and prayed for fear and anxiety to leave.

I had no idea. I had no idea it would be this messy. This hard. Or that it would weave such a beautiful story. And it's only just beginning. It often felt like everything was falling apart. But at the same time everything was coming together.

The picture popped up on my phone, capturing a memory from a year previous. There's a brown-haired girl with her arms outstretched, weighed down by a backpack holding a lot more than books. There's a man by her side. His arms are outstretched too, with a smile across his face so big you wondered why.

That girl was me. The man was Bob Goff. I jumped up

on that stage after he talked because I wanted to be a part of what was written all over his face. I saw something I hadn't recognized in a very long time: joy. It shook me and rattled me and I ran towards it, still wearing the heavy weight of sleepless nights, loneliness, and anxiety. It popped up on my phone after a year. A year since God let me meet joy face to face. A year since He allowed me a glimpse into love. Real love. A year since He slowly began refining me into a brown-haired girl who rediscovered His love and His joy.

It wasn't an easy year. Anxiety and fear and sleeplessness didn't magically go away. But I found that God was faithful and I could trust Him. He never left me alone in the process.

I got home from class and sat down on the floor in my room. In front of me was my Bible, my journal, a pen, and the sun streaming through the window. I flipped open to a blank page and started making a list of all God had brought me through and taught me over the year. I sat there, holding the list in my hand and shaking my head in pure disbelief.

1. He is the One who is enough.
2. He is sufficient.
3. It's not about the applause.
4. The gift-Giver is good.
5. He never left.

It was such a short list and yet I could fit 50 stories under each truth of how God revealed Himself. God knew that would be the year of reclaiming my story—the story He knew all along.

Every time I doubt, I remind myself of this list. Of every moment in the past two years when I believed it was never supposed to be this way. It was through small moments of trusting Jesus and saying yes and showing up anyway that what the enemy meant for destruction, Jesus made for redemption. It was always supposed to be this way.

"Hey," He's whispering. *"I have you right where I want you."*

On the first day of my accounting class, my professor flipped through a slideshow of pictures of her family. After telling us about how much her kids love football and skiing and she and her husband work out at Camp Gladiator together at 5 every morning, she turned off the PowerPoint and came out from behind the podium. Looking across the room at all 75 of her students, she said something I'll never forget.

"I love my family fiercely, but the most important relationship in my life is with Jesus. If His isn't the most important in your life, then come by my office and let me tell you why He should be. There will be a time in your life when things get messy, if they haven't already. Jesus never promised us easy, but He promised hope."

He never promised me easy, but He promised me hope. And that has to be enough.

I've spent the past two years reintroducing myself to love. A different kind of love. A love I no longer needed to earn. A love freely given by Someone who would love me unconditionally. I had received it all my life and yet never looked Him in the eyes before.

I'm still learning. I still have nights where I'd like the switch to turn off my mind so I can sleep. Loneliness still looms over me some days. It's a process. It's not perfect, but I am not the same.

I am not perfect. But I am as free as I've ever been. Free to walk into crowded rooms where I know no one. Free to speak to strangers at Starbucks. Free to be honest. Free to be real.

Free to be loved. Without second-guessing the motive or feeling like love has to be deserved.

My biggest fear has become my biggest freedom.

I want you to know the same freedom too. The freedom to be real and find people that will ask you the same question my professor asked me: "How real are you willing to be?"

The freedom to open your clenched fists and lose control. The freedom to ask the hard questions. The freedom to lay it all out on the table and trust that Jesus isn't going to walk away.

The freedom to leave fear at the door and show up to the

scary things in life and expect that God will show up too. And even when it feels like He's hiding, to show up again.

The freedom to know that He is enough and loves you enough to redeem your story.

The freedom to see joy and not miss Jesus in the people around you. The freedom to speak words of life like confetti.

The freedom to overcome fear.

To become unshakeable.

AFTERWORD

I wrote this letter smack in the middle of everything falling apart. I had forgotten who I was, who God said I was, and who I was meant to be. I wrote this letter for me. But now I think it was meant for you too.

Dear Lauren,

Learn to laugh more, smile bigger, and judge less. Learn to high-five and fist-bump and give hugs. Learn to talk when necessary, but don't let your voice make other voices faint. This life, while it is your life, is not about you. It is about the people you encounter and the encourager you are to them. It is hand-written notes and dancing like no one is watching. It is about the coffee dates and the hard conversations. It is about the time spent investing in others and reaffirming who they are in Christ, and through that you will be affirmed that you are loved and have a purpose in this life. You were made for more, and to some that may look like flying across the globe, but for you it looks a whole lot different. Jesus is using you with every cup of coffee and every phone call and text. Every joy-filled smile and laugh. It is through these things that people will see Jesus—right where you are. While college certainly isn't what you pictured by any means, it's what you've been given, so take it and run with it. What you see is what you get. Maybe this isn't what you've been asking for, but it's what you've been searching for: an environment that needs a real, raw person to show them a real, raw Jesus. You are loved, so go out there and love. Love without judgment and boundaries. Love relentlessly with full pursuit of people. If you are met with love, great. And if you are met with rejection, even better. More room to love. This is what the world needs. And you get the honor of being a part of it. This is your time. Now go out there and take it. This is what I have created you for.

Love doesn't have to be earned.
He never left.
He has the power to redeem your story.
You were made for more.

Goodbye fear.

Hello freedom.

Unshakeable.

ACKNOWLEDGEMENTS

There are so many people who have patiently walked with me through this process. They have fought for me, cried with me, and danced with me. But most importantly, they saw me, knew me, and loved me before this book ever came into existence. They loved me before I ever did anything to impress.

Mom and Dad—Thank you for leading our family with fierce love and a clear pursuit of Jesus. You have believed in me and have poured hundreds of hours into my dreams. I am honored to be your daughter. I love you!

Dad—Dancing with you will forever be one of my greatest joys. Thank you for fighting in the arena with me.

Mom—This is book is 1,000x better because of you. I've learned so much from the way you invite and love the people at your table. I can't wait to read yours one day.

Hannah—May our dance parties and cherry limeades never grow old. Thank you for believing in me. I love you so big.

Conner and Dillon—I am honored to be your sister and cheer you on into the great and amazing things God is calling you to do! Thanks for never taking it easy on me in every wrestling match and on the pitching mound—you've taught me so much courage.

Cheryl and Darrel—Thank you for giving me a seat at your table in Franklin. You loved me fiercely and I can't eat an ice cream bar without thinking of our loud laughter at the dinner table. You've taught me so much about loving people. I don't deserve your kindness.

Trevor, Rebecca, and Nolan—You made me feel loved like no other the moment I stepped off the plane that Sunday afternoon in Nashville. I have never been more thankful for chicken fingers, Little League games, Sunday mornings, rubber ducks, canoes, Mojo's Tacos, and Starbucks drinks—because they all meant time with three of my favorite people. Thank you for loving me so well. Sic 'em Bears.

My incredible editor Ally Fallon—you saw a nineteen-year-old with a dream in her heart and words on her mouth. Thank you for walking with me through this process! You are a gift.

My amazing editor Ashley Scoby—I am forever thankful for your careful eye and help in taking my rough draft and bringing the words to life.

My biggest cheerleaders and the people who teach me more about Jesus every day: Phil, Katie, Becca, Presley, Ashley, DeAnn, Melody, Maggie, Ellie, Sarah, Scott, Jason, Carson,

Greg, and Will. I don't deserve your kindness.

Every friend who has cried, laughed, and encouraged me to press on and keep writing—thank you. You deserve a million confetti poppers for being in my cheering squad. I am so thankful.

I had a lot of dance parties while writing this, but most of them happened while driving down Franklin Road and Mack Hatcher from Mojo's Tacos and blasting Ben Rector's "Old Friends - Live" with one hand waving out my sunroof. It was then that God showed me how to live in freedom.

To you, my reader—I just hope, beyond anything else, you know this God that sees you and knows you and loves you so much.

And to Jesus—it's all for you anyway.

NOTES

1. Tenth Avenue North, "Control," Followers, Provident Label Group LLC, 2016, https://www.youtube.com/watch?v=kFfztu8-bBQ.
2. *Wonder*. Directed by Stephen Chbosky and written by Jack Thorne, Steven Conrad, and Steven Chbosky, Lionsgate, 2017. Script accessed at: https://www.scripts.com/script-pdf/23635
3. 1 Samuel 17:49-50.
4. "All Hail King Jesus," written by Ran Jackson, Peter Mattis, Jeremy Riddle, and Steffany Gretzinger, 2017 Richmond Park Publishing (BMI) / Bethel Music Publishing, see https://bethelmusic.com/chords-and-lyrics/hail-king-jesus/.
5. "U.S. and World Population Clock." United States Census Bureau, U.S. Department of Commerce, www.census.gov/popclock/.

Made in the USA
Columbia, SC
27 April 2020